ART for
Exceptional Children

TRENDS IN ART EDUCATION

Consulting Editor: **Earl Linderman**
Arizona State University

ART FOR EXCEPTIONAL CHILDREN—DONALD UHLIN,
California State University, Sacramento

ALTERNATIVES FOR ART EDUCATION RESEARCH—KENNETH R. BEITTEL,
The Pennsylvania State University

**CHILDREN'S ART JUDGMENT: A CURRICULUM FOR ELEMENTARY ART
APPRECIATION**—GORDON S. PLUMMER,
Murray State University

**ART IN THE ELEMENTARY SCHOOL: DRAWING, PAINTING, AND
CREATING FOR THE CLASSROOM**—MARLENE LINDERMAN,
Arizona State University, Extension Division

EARLY CHILDHOOD ART—BARBARA HERBERHOLZ,
California State University, Sacramento
Extension Division

i

ART for
Exceptional Children

Donald M. Uhlin

Sacramento State College

WM. C. BROWN COMPANY PUBLISHERS
Dubuque, Iowa

Source of figures 86, 89, 90, 91, 92, 93, 121, 122, 123, 184, 185, 186, 187, 196, 197, 198, 199, 200, 201, 202, 203:

Uhlin, D.M.: The Basis of Art for Neurologically Handicapped Children. Figures 2-18. Art Interpretation and Art Therapy, ed. I. Jakab; Psychiatry and Art, Vol. 2. Vth Int. Coll. Psychopathology of Expression, Los Angeles, Cal., 1968; pp. 210-241 (S. Karger, Basel/New York 1969); and

Uhlin, D.M.: The Descriptive Character of Symbol in the Art of a Schizophrenic Girl. Figures 2-5. Art Interpretation and Art Therapy, ed. I. Jakab; Psychiatry and Art, Vol. 2. Vth Int. Coll. Psychopathology of Expression, Los Angeles, Cal., 1968; pp. 242-248 (S. Karger, Basel/New York 1969).

To my father

contents

Preface   ix

PART ONE
Theory of Personality and Art

1. **Structuring and Maintaining Reality   3**

   What Is Reality?   3
   The Human Personality as Center   4
   Communication Through Somatic Function   5
   Significance of Body-Image Projection   8
   Symbol in History and Personality   10
   Summary   17

2. **Development of the Normal Child in Art   18**

   Basic Theories of Child Art   18
   Significance of Drawing Forms in Early Childhood   25
   Aesthetic Quality and Spatial Organization   33
   Schematic Storytelling   39
   The Social Self-Concept of the Older Child   43
   Summary   46

PART TWO
Art for the Exceptional Child

3. **The Mentally Deficient Personality in Art   51**

   Definition and Classification of Mental Deficiency   51
   Mentally Deficient Art Expression   52
   Strategies for Enriched Experiencing Through Art   56

4. **The Physically Impaired Child and Art   64**

   The Child with an Orthopedic Handicap   64
   The Neurologically Handicapped Child   68
      Understanding Dysfunction Through Drawing   70
      Effects of Medical Therapy on NH Art   76
      Therapy Through Art Material Strategies   84
   The Child with a Visual Impairment   88
   The Child with an Auditory Impairment   90

5. **Art and the Emotionally Disturbed Child   94**

   Etiology of Emotional Disturbance in the Child   95
   Emotional Disturbance and Art Expression   96
      The Circle   96
      The Cross   103
      The Rectangle   114
   Art and Psychotherapy for the Emotionally Disturbed   126
      The Case of Mary   126

6. **Case Examples of Multiple Impairment   131**

   Jimmy, Fifteen Years   131
   Judy, Eight Years   135

Index   141

An exceptional child was once observed in the activity of drawing a man taking his dog for a walk, but in his drawing the dog appeared to be at least twice the size of the man. After short inquiry the child stated, "Well, dogs *are* nicer than people!" Many of us, to be sure, have felt this same way at moments after we have encountered some unpleasantness with another person. Ralph Waldo Emerson once said, "The more I see of men, the more I appreciate my dog." Seldom, however, are many of us able to bring such experiencing to this essence of statement. Most often it is the artist or the child who holds this deeper view or insight concerning the world and who appears capable of such expression. Through this discussion of the exceptional child, we anticipate that his art may provide a view of the world that is not so totally unreal or distorted from our own. Perhaps, to the contrary, we will find it often provides a glimpse of a deeper truth.

Once we recognize and understand the keys to the child through the mirror we call art, we will be capable of empathizing with his view. Then the exceptional child, whose behavior is at the first perplexing, and even bizarre, will no longer be considered too distant from any one of us. It is important to reduce the unfamiliar character of human needs, for we *cannot* respond to needs we do not recognize and we *will not* respond to needs we do not feel. Above all, we must gain a proper respect for the child. Robert Henri once said, "Do not feel superior to the child, for you are not!" It may be assumed that this comment includes the exceptional child, for he too holds the image of God. How few of us respect each other in this regard today! Much of our hatred and bitterness and disregard for each other would vanish once we could attain to such a proper attitude. Even the child previously mentioned, and Emerson as well, in a typically human way regard the behavior of man rather than his true status. *All* children carry the stamp of the Creator and in turn reproduce their own natural self-image when they draw. Corrado Ricci, the nineteenth-century Italian poet, once wrote, "The sacred Scriptures tell us that the eternal Father finished His work by the creation of man. With the creation of man, on the contrary, the children begin theirs."* It will be observed, without exception, that *all* children draw a human figure as their first representational form. So it is beyond comprehension, and yet obvious to the heart, that these whom we may consider to be the least do also carry our utmost respect and optimism. May the teacher, the social worker, and the psychiatrist never underestimate the status of the child we are to consider, for we are all alike to a far greater degree than we are dissimilar.

In this work we will note that the difficulty adults have in understanding the child is due, in large measure, to our different mode of experiencing. We have lost the naïve but profound bases of physical and emotional referencing which are primary to most young children and to exceptional children generally. We tend to rationalize those experiences which have physical and emotional origin, and thus we negate or deny those very roots which provide the essence of meaning for the child. In our discussion we will concern ourselves with the multitude of interrelationships regarding the physical, emotional, and rational forces with which the individual forms his reality. Perhaps we will again be able, in some small way, to seek and find that greater discern-

*Corrado Ricci, *L'arte Dei Bambini*, Bologna, 1887. Reproduced in *Pedagogical Sem.*, vol. 3, 1894, pp. 302-307.

ment of meaning in life by studying and aiding the child. Establishing sensitivity in and through material experiences will form the basis of our general procedure for art teaching and therapy. The life of the individual will not be seen in the context of his quantitative acquisition of knowledge—we will leave such a premise to others. Our view will consider his qualitative experience and its expression in art. That shall be our contribution.

PART ONE Theory of Personality and Art

Structuring and Maintaining Reality 1

Since our attention regarding the exceptional child is to focus upon his human needs, as reflected and resolved through his art, we must first consider the process of human reality structuring and maintenance generally—and then the basic principles in art process which characteristically make art a reflectory instrument. In the following chapter the development of the normal child will be reviewed as a pattern of such process and for the purpose of establishing a background against which we will then discuss the exceptional child.

What Is Reality?

They said, 'You have a blue guitar,
You do not play things as they are.'
The man replied, 'Things as they are
Are changed upon the blue guitar.'[1]

—Wallace Stevens

When we engage ourselves in reading, we are in that very act involved in a process which may best be called *reality structuring*. This process is initiated by sensory contact with an outer material environment which deeper physical, emotional, and rational centers receive and interpret. From the communicated experience a response is then formed and transmitted back through the body to complete the behavioral cycle.

In the past, the so-called "behaviorists" have stated and oversimplified clarification of this process by stimulus-response theory. Their treatment of reality structuring considers man's personality on a mechanical-animal level, and were we to take their position, we would be forced to consider all meaning on a purely temporal stratum. Full understanding of personality function would under such conditions be ignored, and our discussion would be restricted by the relative character of both time and space. We would eventually become existentialists or nihilists who abundantly are evidenced to be living out their despair in our present day. The two factors mentioned, time and space, clarify the limitations of any such temporal or "temporary" reality, and we are immediately encouraged by such definition, of a transient reality, to look beyond surface experiencing to view things in a deeper meaning. Our first interest, then, is to broaden our scope of thought in discussing man's experience, for it alone determines his process of reality structuring.

We must recognize that most people in this world do not generally "see" through and beyond the dark glass of materialism. They cannot even start to imagine experiencing a reality where space is endless and time does not exist. Indeed, the very thought of such a prospect may leave them a bit frightened. Perhaps, however, our initial difficulty is that most of us do not even begin to

1. Wallace Stevens, *The Man with the Blue Guitar* (New York: Alfred A. Knopf, Inc., 1952), p. 3. Printed by permission.

consider such possibilities due to our constant struggle in the fast-moving day-to-day drama of life. And more often than not the meanings we find in this volatile materialism are only connotations derived from mere surface recognition. We will find as we deal further with this subject that the essence of reality is most certainly found in an understanding of deeper meanings and that material reality is essentially a symbolic reference when compared to these meanings.

In attempting to catch this deeper glimmer of meaning, we must consider ourselves "removed to a place apart" where we may seek a new perspective of the whole action and examine the circumstances within which we structure our reality.

Material reality from such a distance is found to be organized from substance which is basically energy subjugated to the bonds of time and space. Matter, according to Einstein, is energy caught in a unique balance of space and time. We may say, therefore, that unseen energy is the essence of material which we perceive with our physical senses. We may as well consider this clarification of the nature of material reality to be analogous to the nature of man, for he is similarly composed. His essence is found in the spiritual component of his being which we refer to here as *personality*. As the spiritual facet of the person, the personality is bound *to* and expresses itself *through* a material body.

Man is most readily recognized as a part of temporal reality by the physical component of his person. Usually we speak of this physical component as the *body*; but in a more technical language it is called *soma*, and its activity is referred to as *somatic function*. Often we tend to consider a man's soma to be the man but, of course, in essence it is not, for the center of man's reality must always be regarded in terms of his awareness of self. Such self-awareness lies within and is the basic characteristic of personality. Physical experiencing of a physical environment, on the other hand, indicates to us that the soma is basically a communication center which connects the personality with temporal reality. It is a house of clay to which the personality is limited while dwelling therein. Our stress upon somatic function in later discussion will help us recognize that the condition and purpose of the soma must not be overlooked. Its appearance, on the other hand, is usually overstressed.

The Human Personality as Center

Generally when we speak of personality, we are referring to expression determined by the interaction of functions which we place under the labels of *mind, emotion,* and *will*. This is the "heart" of the individual, and yet we must not confuse it with his physical heart, just as we must not confuse the mind of a man with his physical brain. They are as distinctly and essentially different as the spiritual is different from the physical and the heavenly from the earthly.

The human personality has a *rational function* which we most often consider in the word *thinking*. This is descriptive of *mind*. Emotion, in like manner, we consider in the word *feeling*, but it may more properly be regarded as the *affective function*. *Will* is the *responsive function*, and because it ultimately determines behavior, we often consider it the core of the human personality.

It is important here to note that the human mind functions on two levels: a large unconscious operation and a smaller conscious operation. For our later purposes it is also significant that while the conscious level carries with it the dominant sexual identification of the individual, the unconscious level, in contrast, holds a contrasexual image. Thus in the dominant masculine personality we have an opposite sexual image which is of a feminine character. It is the "mother" in the man and is referred to by Carl Jung as the *anima*. In the woman

PERSONALITY

Center
of
Reality
and
Self-Awareness

Functions:

Thinking—Mind
Feeling—Emotion
Responding—Will

is found a "father" which he refers to as the *animus.* The rabbit hole in *Alice's Adventures in Wonderland* symbolically describes the devouring female characteristic of the anima. The implication of such an imagery, of course, is that the story takes place "underground" or in the unconscious mind. Poe uses a similar image of the threatening feminine unconscious in the subject of a terrible whirlpool in his story *A Descent into the Maelstrom.* In like manner, the animus of the woman in art and literature is often seen as a horse emerging and disappearing into a mist or hole (fig. 1). In this role the horse is often associated with the more primitive unconscious.

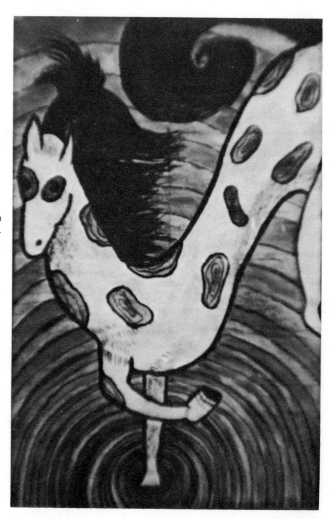

Figure 1. "Horse." Tempera painting by girl 16 years.

In summary we must note that man is created in a unity with the body; he is a body and a personality, but the personality, like a vapor, is not bound to remain. Perhaps this fact, among other reasons, is why the butterfly, with its erratic flight, is the symbolical equivalent of the personality or soul.

Communication Through Somatic Function

The human personality is like the vacuum space of a container. It appears from birth to be just waiting to feel, to know, and to respond. We may best look upon the human soma, or body, as the container itself—it is the most immediate environment for the human personality, and anything which will become a part of the individual's reality must, of necessity, be experienced in and through the container itself.

One of man's most distorted viewpoints is that regarding his own body. He constantly lavishes much of his time on it by exercising it, feeding it, combing it, dressing it, and sleeping it. Too often it ends up being worshipped and served rather than fulfilling him by serving him. After all, what possible good is it to him or to anyone else once he finally leaves it? If we are to view the body properly, we must see it as a means to an end and not as an end in itself. We are not essentially our physical body, but it is given to us to care for properly that we might experience in the deepest and fullest respect.

While man is restricted to his body, it is the sole means for him to experience, structure, and maintain temporal reality which we note is characterized by motion. Time and space, of course, are the factors producing what we call motion. The material of temporal reality, in turn, will provide a basis for meanings found outside of the space-time reference. Such meanings will be discussed briefly at the end of this chapter.

The senses of the body provide a communicative function, and we may state that the body, then, is the physical counterpart in the total process of perception. Experiences communicated to the personality through the body are initially, and for the most part unconsciously, registered. Some experiencing is never brought to a conscious level of awareness in the mind, but it may be expressed almost entirely on a physical-emotional level. This is most often the case for exceptional children and for younger children generally. For instance, as adults how consciously aware are most of us of our bodily positioning or even of our weight on our feet? It is a very meaningful experience, but too often we do not consciously recognize such a fact until it is altered by our riding up or down in an elevator. Unconscious as most of our bodily experiencing is, it is the one source through which we constantly structure and maintain ourselves in temporal reality.

Postural status, the constant positioning and repositioning of the body, is meaningful and essential for the security we all find necessary in order to maintain ourselves. The creative personality may often be viewed as a person who identifies well in and through the body—who is very secure in himself and therefore highly flexible emotionally. Steinmetz, the electrical genius, is said to have once been asked to fix a huge dynamo, and in response he brought in a cot and slept next to the machine for several days. He then calculated and reported the necessary repairs. He had felt the vibrations of the motor in his body and could empathize sufficiently to accurately determine the need. In contrast, we often find that the exceptional child, and the normal individual generally, lacks the ability to transmit in a rational manner that same bodily sensitivity. Also, the exceptional child may receive distortions of somatic information due to some impairment within his own body.

Reality must always be viewed as dependent upon the interrelationship of the personality and the body. Through the interaction of the personality and the body, an image of one's self is constantly constructed and destroyed. Such a self-view is called *body-image*. A proper concept of body-image is basic to our later discussion of projection in art.

It is significant for our later discussion to note that the soma, or body, does serve the personality and cannot voluntarily withdraw from it of its own accord. A portion may, of course, be blocked or cut off due to injury, or the function may be distorted due to injury or illness. The personality, on the other hand, with a tremendous conceptual image mass, may of its own effort withdraw any distance from the body. Such an extreme act of detachment is best labeled

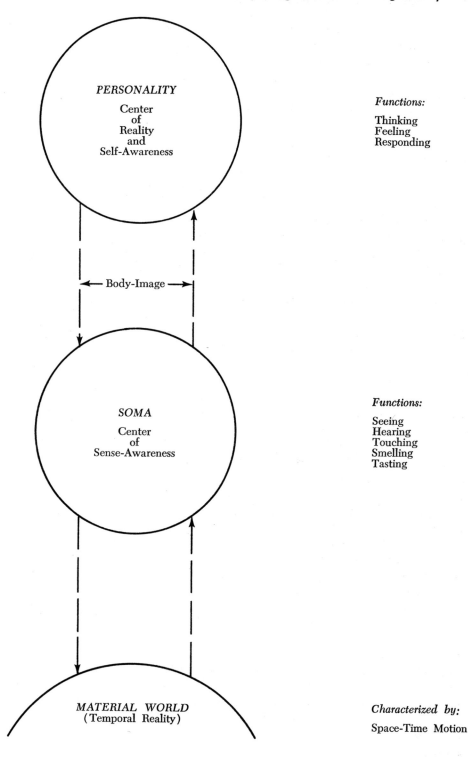

disassociation. In the event of this occurring, we are dealing with psychopatho-logical circumstances which in common terms may be called a psychic suicide or "mental breakdown." The break is actually emotional *and* mental, as the conflict affects both the feeling and the thinking functions. The healthy personality strongly holds material reality in view as a gestalt configuration by building and maintaining constantly from the multitude of interactions of the personality, the body, and the material world.

Significance of Body-Image Projection

In dealing with art as a total reflective device for the life of the individual, we must first recognize how art allows us to stand where another has stood to see him as he expresses himself. The key to such significance in art may basically be found in what we have already referred to as body-image.

Let us recall here that body-image is not purely from the somatic reference or from the personality reference but that *it is a gestalt image of self produced through the interaction of both the physiological and personality components as they function to structure and maintain reality.* Paul Schilder called body-image "the tri-dimensional image everybody has about himself."[1] Sir Henry Head, an eminent physiologist before the time of Schilder, stressed the somatic function in body-image and referred to a "postural model of the body" or "schemata."[2] Others have discussed the body-image with emphasis upon the psychological functions, but we must reemphasize that we are not primarily interested in a definition on a conceptual level, with somatic or psychic emphasis, but rather we are interested in the implied meanings found in the total body-image function as it is expressed in art.

The implied meanings in body-image are both symbolic and organic since they are expressed from respective psychic and somatic functions. Due to the interaction just mentioned, we note that these meanings, in projected form in art, make up a composite self-view. Indeed, it is malfunction or loss of interaction of either the psychic or somatic component which provides a clue to pathology in art expression. Evaluation of psychopathology in art will be available according to the sensitivity and insight of the individual who is utilizing spontaneous art productions or a projective drawing tool as found in the House-Tree-Person Test. An "open view" of the total state of the subject, in regard to both somatic and psychic functions, may be seen by the trained observer. Herbert Read has stated in regard to this:

> . . . art is deeply involved in the actual process of perception, thought and bodily action. It is not so much a governing principle to be applied to life, as a governing mechanism which can only be ignored at our peril.[3]

When a person draws a human figure, or a related configuration such as the house or tree, he projects his personal body-image with all of its somatic and psychical meanings. The physical view of one's self is most readily discernible in such a projection as simple comparison often brings immediate visual corroboration. Puppet construction is an interesting activity from this point of view, for the producer works quite unconsciously and fails to recognize the projective factor (fig. 2). In most of these projections the body-image includes the subject's hair and eye coloring, and some females may spend considerable time mixing paint to produce the exact color for painting a mouth which will correspond to their own lipstick. Of even more significance, however, are the subtle exaggerations of form which reflect a phenomenal sensitivity to the basic structure and spatial extension of the body mass.

Psychical function in the body-image projection is clearly evident in the puppet's role, as the puppet first appears, and then later behaves, in a puppet production. The female usually projects a generally passive role in such sub-

---

1. Paul Schilder, *The Image and Appearance of the Human Body* (New York: International Universities Press, Inc., 1950), p. 11.
2. Sir Henry Head, *Aphasia and Kindred Disorders of Speech*, vol 1 (New York: Hafner Publishing Co., 1963), p. 488.
3. Herbert Read, *Education Through Art*, p. 14.

Figure 2. Bag puppet and the highly creative artist-teacher who produced it. She is confined to a wheelchair due to a polio disability.

jects as a rabbit, a squirrel, or a cat, while the masculine personality produces a tough bandit, a prize fighter, or a wolf. Such roles are, of course, described by many individual exaggerations and delineations which, while symbolical, produce an overall character. Drawings will be found to be identical to the puppet in the projected characteristics, but often the individual will more readily construct a puppet than draw a person due to the greater "distance" of unconscious projection in the puppet.

In puppet construction the effect of somatic variation on the personality is evidenced many times by respective physical irregularity or an unusual role regarding the puppet. A young girl whose face was covered with smallpox scars was noted to construct an "Ugly Duckling" puppet—a clear expression of the somatic state interacting with, and hence affecting, the personality in the projected body-image. Such expression is simply due to the unique character of the body-image and again indicates that art, as a projective expression, is a wonderful mirror of the inner self-view.

Throughout this work the H-T-P Test will be utilized as a basic drawing reference. Its application is rapid and economical, and it is a valuable tool as a screening device or as a part of psycho-diagnostic test batteries in the case of individuals. The test is administered by giving the subject 8½-by-11-inch white drawing paper and a No. 2 pencil with eraser. On separate sheets of paper the subject is instructed to draw a house, a tree, and a person. Often, with children, the Drawing of the Family is added for further insight. Protocols for the test will not be discussed separately here but may be found in a great body of other available literature. Our purpose is simply to describe the operating principles upon which such tests are founded while we discuss the needs of the exceptional child.

Symbol in History and Personality

In the Book of Proverbs we read, "The spirit of man is the candle of the Lord, searching all the inward parts of the belly." We may say that the spirit component of man is, therefore, the center of God-consciousness and a means of communication with transcendent reality, just as the physical body is a means of communication with material reality. The communication of the spirit, however, must be understood to be in regard to *meanings* which are spiritual. The previously discussed factors of physical experience provide the concept basis through which spiritual meanings are discerned. Thus we may say the "inward parts of the belly," as the physical concept basis, must be searched by the spirit itself to discern meanings of symbolic character. John Chrystostom once said,

> If man had been incorporeal, God would have given him purely incorporeal gifts; but since his soul is joined to a body, things suprasensible are ministered to him by means of sensible things.[4]

In determining meaning in reality structuring we must ask, "Is seeing believing or is believing 'seeing'?" The spiritual "seeing" we are discussing assumes symbolic meaning in physical content, *for the language of the spirit is the symbol.* This is most logical, for we recognize that symbols are not dependent upon the space and time characteristics of temporal relationships. All temporal life experiences, on the other hand, are symbolical when we view them from the spiritual level. As we shall see, real meanings in life are found when we understand temporal experiences on the spiritual level through the language of the symbol.

For matters of clarification of function we have categorically separated the personality and the *spirit* of man. When the components are united, as many people prefer, they would best be spoken of as *psychical.* Some would even prefer to consider spirit a function of the personality. While this would be acceptable in most discussion, we prefer here to differentiate the two in order to clarify the functions involved for the communication of experiencing in reality structuring.

It is evident from our discussion that the temporal reality of the material world and the spiritual reality of the symbol both communicate initially to the unconscious level of awareness in the mind. However, there is far greater tendency for temporal experiences to rise to consciousness—and be recognized for what they are on their surface level of meaning—than for their symbolical significance to become evident. Most often the spiritual implications of the experience are, therefore, only unconsciously "known." This fact, of course, implies the danger of symbolic content to the mind—something the advertising man is well aware of in taking advantage of us. We should be careful regarding the choice of experiences with which we decide to populate our minds.

Further, and especially pertinent for our later considerations, is recognition of the mind as the center of a battlefield for psychic identification and acceptance. It is here that the hermaphroditic "gods" of the anima and animus wage their warfare and the individual's "old man" or "old woman" threatens the field

---

4. Cited by F. E. Hulme in *Symbolism in Christian Art*, p. 5.

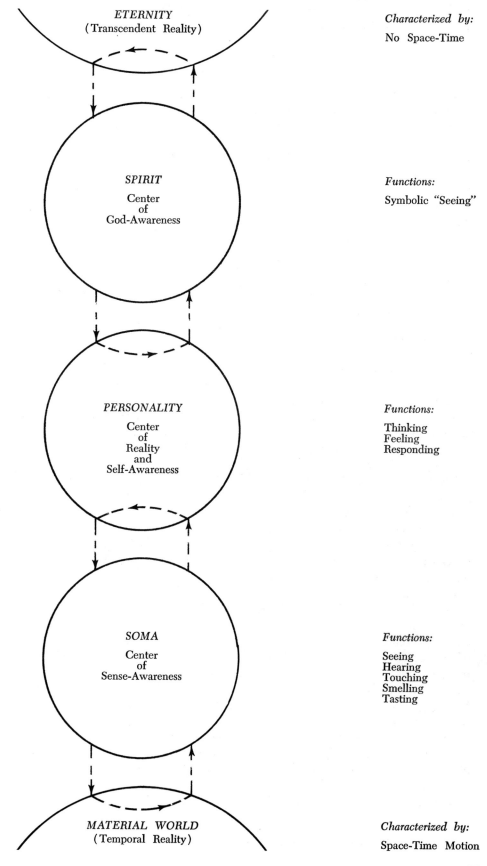

ETERNITY
(Transcendent Reality)

Characterized by:
No Space-Time

SPIRIT
Center
of
God-Awareness

Functions:
Symbolic "Seeing"

PERSONALITY
Center
of
Reality
and
Self-Awareness

Functions:
Thinking
Feeling
Responding

SOMA
Center
of
Sense-Awareness

Functions:
Seeing
Hearing
Touching
Smelling
Tasting

MATERIAL WORLD
(Temporal Reality)

Characterized by:
Space-Time Motion

of consciousness. The conscious mind performs a censorship function for unacceptable facts by forcing them into the unconscious. Often, however, the process of art or dreams will indicate the manner in which they attempt to force themselves back into some degree of consciousness.

A dream may be very vivid in its imagery but be "lost" the moment one becomes fully conscious. In an attempt to recapture the unconscious factor, we often seek to return to the sleeping state to "finish" or resolve the image. We fail to actually bring the dream to consciousness, but even if we were to be successful in the attempt, it would remain on a purely symbolic level. As such it would continue to hold its fascinating and puzzling character. Such a course of events is to be expected, and we must now understand the dream more deeply to see the spiritual communication conveyed through its symbolic imagery.

Dreams are symbolical. They are most probably static images which, at the moment of awakening, are fused together into the characteristic motion of consciousness. The example of Alfred Maury's famous dream is a case in point. Maury dreamed himself a subject of the French Revolution who was sent to the guillotine after having been tried and convicted. His dream, however, appeared to be obvious instantaneous reaction formed from the physical shock of the bedrail, just above his head, falling across his neck, thus triggering the dream by the culminating sensation of the guillotine blade on his neck.

It was Maury who attempted to indicate that all dreams have a physical origin. Subsequent study, however, has suggested that dreams are of at least three sources of origin. These three levels correspond to the three components of man: soma, personality, and spirit.

The first, the *somatic dream,* is clarified by Isaiah:

> It shall even be as when an hungry man dreameth, and behold, he eateth; but he awaketh and his soul is empty; or as when a thirsty man dreameth, and behold, he drinketh; but he awaketh, and behold, he is faint, and his soul hath appetite . . .

This statement describes well the physically based dream. The real bodily need in such a case activates the memory images leading to satisfaction in the unconscious mind.

A second type of dream may be called a *soul dream.* In this type of dream the human personality attempts to work out in unconscious symbolism a successful conclusion or "fulfillment" of that which in conscious life is a basis of difficulty and anxiety. Jeremiah in regarding false prophets speaks of this type of dream as "your dreams which ye cause to be dreamed." Most people recognize the matter of wish fulfillment and problem-solving in such dreams. It is logical that such activity should not only be sought and continued in sleep, but that it also should be more highly "colored" and enhanced. Anxieties, as found in such dreams, are often symbolically expressed in sufficient clarity to provide an excellent basis for counseling. A young woman, for instance, who was greatly in fear of pregnancy spoke from the following dream reference in a counseling session:

> I found myself opening the hall door which leads down into the basement. The entire basement was filled with a huge plastic bag in which two bear cubs were fighting over vegetables on the floor. I slammed the door in fear knowing that when they finished the vegetables they would come upstairs and raise havoc.

This dream appears immediately to be bizarre but actually holds only a thin disguise over conscious recognition in the mind. The door is the entrance to the womb as signified in the image of the basement. The plastic bag is the amniotic sac, while the bear cubs are obviously two fetal infants nourished within the mother. The woman fears that their birth will bring a mental-emotional disturbance as expressed in the phrase "havoc upstairs."

The third type of dream, the *spirit dream,* is the most difficult to clarify because of its origin outside of that which Jung calls the "biological substrate." These dreams tend to evade rational examination because they are transcendent in nature and origin. They come *upon* men, and Jung's attempt to explain them in terms of "synchronism" is a fine bit of German rationalism which only serves to bring out his essential pantheism. Our text will disagree with him from the basis of his existentialist view as we would also disagree with the views of Kant in like manner, though we do use the word *transcendent* for lack of a better term. In contrast to the Jungian view is the view of Biblical theology which says that the dream comes upon men from the outside personage of God.

From the dream, and from art as well, we may say that symbol is the one truly universal language. While the experience upon which it is based enters through the senses, it is basically spiritual in character. The fact that art communicates meanings across the time and cultural barriers of history reveals and verifies the spiritual character of symbol. Cirlot states:

> . . . symbolism adds a new value to an object or an act, without violating its immediate or 'historical' validity. Once it is brought to bear, it turns the object or action into an 'open' event. . . .[5]

He further states:

> The symbolist meaning of a phenomenon helps explain these 'intimate reasons,' since it links the instrumental with the spiritual, the human with the cosmic, the casual with the causal, disorder with order, and since it justifies a word like universe which, without these wiser implications, would be meaningless. . . .[6]

That man is ministered to through the symbol is evident, and symbol is therefore basically anthropomorphic—spiritual but in man-form. Consequently, the symbol has a perfect continuity of meaning on the archetypal level. Jules Le Belle states:

> . . . every created object is, as it were, a reflection of Divine perfection, a natural and perceptible sign of a supernatural truth.[7]

Because man is created in the image of God, the "prints" reflect the "Imprinter." Symbol is innately a part of man's being. In final analysis we must agree with Cirlot:

> This language of images and emotions is based, then, upon a precise and crystallized means of expression, revealing transcendent truths, external to man. . . .[8]

While some variation of meaning will undoubtedly occur within the context of the individual's personal and social reference, archetypal levels of meaning remain consistent. No one teaches the child that the sun is the God-Father image. The symbolism is inherent to the child's spiritual awareness. In figure 3 we note how wonderfully a child utilizes the archetypal symbolic meaning of

5. J. E. Cirlot, *A Dictionary of Symbols,* p. xiv.
6. Ibid., p. xiii.
7. Ibid., cited by Cirlot, p. xxx.
8. Ibid.

the sun to tell the story of Cain and Abel. The sacrifice of Abel is received by God through the image of the smoke rising, while Cain's sacrifice is rejected in the returning smoke, due to its bloodless character. No question need be asked regarding the sun as a symbol for God.

Figure 3. "Cain and Abel" by boy 7 years.

In figure 4 we note how a five-year-old child represents the family—three flowers for the three children and a large sun for the strong father-image. The mother in this family was institutionalized, and the father was raising the children by himself.

Mother may be symbolized in dreams or art by the moon, water, a house, or a mountain. Ground, in a general sense, is one of the most common symbols for mother. We all have heard of the mother in the following Mother Goose rhyme:

> There was an old woman lived under the hill
> If she hasn't moved she lives there still
> Baked apples she sold and cranberry pies
> And she's the old woman who never tells lies.

This description is simply typical of the earth mother-image most mothers provide for the child. Such a mother loves and nourishes, she never lies, and of course never changes in the eyes of the child. Figure 5 provides a contrast to this image. To this eleven-year-old boy, the mother is cold and dominant; the father is weak and ineffective. The boy himself, in the self-image of a tree, tries to rise above the mother but often is defeated as is indicated in the drooping foliage. His further attempt to defend or separate himself from the mother is evidenced in the fence.

Figure 4. Painting by boy 5 years

Figure 5. Landscape drawing by boy 11 years

While the tree may often be an image of self, it may be an image of mother as well if the individual is highly bound up with and dependent upon the mother (fig. 6). In figure 7 the same type of squirrel's hole is seen, but along with that dependency form, this sixteen-year-old boy indicates his close association to mother by placing his small, effeminate house next to hers. The mother who overprotects and absorbs the personality of her boy may well produce a "flower" that will have much difficulty experiencing in future years.

Figure 6. Tree drawing by boy 10 years.

Figure 7. House and Tree drawing by boy 16 years.

Summary

A foundation for understanding and discussing the individual through his art has now been established. We understand that every child structures a reality through the total interaction of physical and psychical components: the soma, the personality, and the spirit. The soma and spirit are communicative components for the establishment of reality in the personality. Sensory communication of temporal reality is provided by the body, while symbolic meaning, concerning transcendent reality, is communicated by the spirit. The mirror of art may act as a reflection of any or all of these functions due to the projective character of the art process. Further discussion will now clarify how education is essentially purposed to motivate and sensitize the child for a higher degree of qualitative experiencing in the process of reality structuring. In a deeper sense this may be considered therapy for the exceptional child.

References

BIELIAUSKAS, V. J. *The House-Tree-Person Research Review*. Beverly Hills, Calif.: Western Psychological Services, 1965.

BUCK, JOHN. *The House-Tree-Person Technique: Revised Manual*. Beverly Hills, Calif.: Western Psychological Services, 1966.

CIRLOT, J. E. *A Dictionary of Symbols*. London: Routledge and Kegan Paul, Ltd., 1962.

HAMMER, EMANUEL. *The Clinical Application of Projective Drawings*. Springfield, Ill.: Charles C Thomas, Publisher, 1958.

——— *The H-T-P Clinical Research Manual*. Beverly Hills, Calif.: Western Psychological Services, 1955.

HEAD, HENRY. *Aphasia and Kindred Disorders of Speech*. New York: Hafner Publishing Co., Inc., 1963.

Holy Bible. King James Version. London: Oxford University Press.

HULME, F. E. *Symbolism in Christian Art*. New York: The Macmillan Co., 1899.

JOLLES, ISAAC. *A Catalogue for the Qualitative Interpretation of the House-Tree-Person*. Beverly Hills, Calif.: Western Psychological Services, 1964.

JUNG, CARL. *Psyche and Symbol*. New York: Doubleday Anchor, 1958.

KOCH, CHARLES. *The Tree Test*. New York: Grune and Stratton, Inc., 1952.

MACHOVER, KAREN. *Personality Projection in the Drawing of the Human Figure*. Springfield, Ill.: Charles C Thomas, Publisher, 1949.

READ, HERBERT. *Education Through Art*. New York: Pantheon Books, Inc., 1958.

SCHILDER, PAUL. *The Image and Appearance of the Human Body*. New York: International Universities Press, 1950.

2 Development of the Normal Child in Art

Now that we have a basic understanding of the process of reality structuring and maintenance, we will turn our attention to the manner in which the typical normal child experiences in and through art. Such an identification on our part is a necessary premise for comparison when we later consider the exceptional child. In regarding the development of the normal child in art, a brief résumé of theoretical background will be considered before our attention is directed to developmental characteristics in their chronological setting.

Basic Theories of Child Art

The first research concerning child art was initiated in the winter of 1882 when Corrado Ricci, an Italian poet, observed the drawings of children under an archway where he had sought shelter from a sudden downpour of rain. His reports encouraged the study of art expression as a means for more deeply understanding the total experiencing of the child. The Child Study Era at the turn of the century was a movement of world magnitude and centered upon the behavioral patterns of the child at each step in his development. International congresses were formed in those years to pool data and structure theories which would communicate just what it was that the child was resolving at a particular chronological age. By 1920 a rather clear idea of the "stages of growth" in artistic development had evolved from this study, and attention was centering upon tests of measurement for specific behavioral aptitudes. As the century progressed, other fields of inquiry formed and had a great influence upon our present understanding of child development in art. Prominent among them were the gestalt and psychoanalytic schools in psychology. It is imperative for our later discussion that we lay hold of the broad implications which this historical body of research presents.

Ricci noted in his observations that the child starts drawing with an "interlacing network of lines" and then moves on to simple representational forms which become more detailed with age. He recognized in these simple forms that the child draws a description of the subject according to his knowledge of that subject and not according to its visual appearance. This "mental concept" consideration of the young child's drawing characterized all of the very early studies. It is emphasized, moreover, in another of Ricci's observations in which he speaks of the child drawing a sexton ascending the bell tower visible through the walls of the building. Such an "x-ray" view suggests that children not only draw their idea of the subject but that they also draw that which is most important. If the inside is more important than the outside, then the outside, or exterior, is made transparent or left off completely.

A number of the early studies, especially those by Lichtwark (1887) and Baldwin (1898) attempted to find parallels between the child's development in drawing and the evolutionary theories which were popular at the time. The development of the child in art was compared in the early years to paleolithic cave drawings, with the notion in mind that the child would progress in his life through all of the sequential stages of mankind. For many years anthropologists and psychologists drained this idea from every possible angle. It did have the effect of giving rise to an interest in the "stages" of development in child art.

In 1892 James Sully, an English philosopher and psychologist, published his *Studies of Childhood* in which he used the term *schemata* or *schema* for the child's simplified drawing concept. His work, highly influenced by Ricci, placed emphasis upon the simple plan or mental concept of the child which represents the subject rather than rendering it in its visual likeness. We find from this definition that the word *schema*, in referring to the child's drawing, always suggests a simple representational symbol which stands for the subject. It is composed of shapes and lines of a singular and direct character.

Earl Barnes was perhaps the first researcher to really organize, conduct, and report scholarly studies of child art. In 1893, in reporting on child drawing responses to a story motivation, he noted that a definite sequence of development occurred according to chronological age. He found, also, that figures in the drawings often changed from a frontal view to a profile view at nine years of age. In regarding the young child's art, he considered it generally to be a basic symbolic language.

In 1895 Louise Maitland found that young children had a decided preference for drawing the human figure. This observation had earlier been made by Ricci and is substantiated by many later studies.

The first description of developmental stages according to chronological age was given by Herman Lukens in 1896:

1. Scribbling (to 4 years).
2. The Golden Age—The child blends story and picture (4 to 8 years).
3. The Critical Period—The child's judgment of his art stagnates his efforts (9 to 14 years).
4. Period of Rebirth—Creative power and artistic development for a few (14 years on).

In 1902 Arthur B. Clark used an apple with a hatpin stuck through it as a device for studying children's attitudes toward an object in drawing (fig. 8). He found that ninety-seven percent of the six-year-olds drew the whole pin as if the apple were transparent. The younger children were therefore emphasized again to be conceptual in drawing. By nine years of age the majority of the children stopped the pin at the edge of the apple.

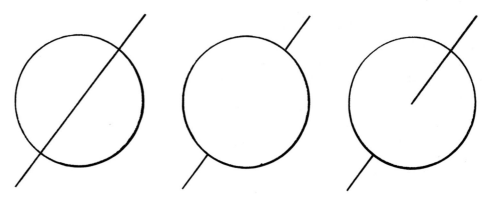

Figure 8. The Apple and Hatpin (after A. B. Clark). Three stages from pure concept to pure percept are represented.

In 1904 Sigfried Levenstein of Leipzig used the term "storytelling" to describe the young child's art. In the early years he noted that it was "fragmentary," and we could probably best interpret that to mean disunified on the spatial surface of the paper. He observed that the older child used a storytelling which involved linear, panoramic, and time-sequence factors. The general term *storytelling* is an excellent description of the vivid manner in which the child expresses, through his concepts, in art.

The terms *ideoplastic* and *physioplastic* were used by Max Verworn in 1907 to describe the child's art development. Ideoplastic refers to ideas and regards the apperceptive process more than direct sensory experiencing. The symbolists or expressionists in art would be classified ideoplastic artists. Physioplastic refers to the individual's relationship to his physical environment as experienced through the senses. Impressionistic art would fit within this classification. His stages regarding the child's art development were basically as follows:

1. Unconscious Physioplastic Stage—Scribbling (to 4 years).
2. Unconscious Ideoplastic Stage—Symbols used to express ideas (4 to 9 years).
3. Conscious Ideoplastic vs. Physioplastic—The growing intellect vs. sensitivity of physical maturation (9 to 13 years).
4. Conscious Physioplastic Expression—Wins out in the adolescent period. Physical experiencing of materials must therefore be the emphasis while the intelligence aids in guiding these sensibilities.

In 1908 William Stern expressed a view that the child experiences himself as the center of space in his drawing and that he gradually attempts to subordinate his environment to himself. This observation will later aid us in understanding what motivates the child in his need to highly organize the space of the drawing surface. Stern also noted a relationship between drawing development and language development. He states, "Scribbling is to drawing much what babbling is to speech."

Through his experiences with children in his special art classes, Franz Cizek, the first teacher to actually sensitize children to a subject through art, came to speak of the earliest drawings as "smearings" and the later schematic representations as *abstract-symbolic* productions. He recognized that the drawings of young children are simplified representative forms standing for the subject. Perhaps his best biographer is Viola who describes in detail the wonderful verbal interchange through which Cizek extended the child's reference of experience and thus sensitized the child emotionally and rationally to the subject.

In 1921 Cyril Burt came out with a full and highly acceptable description of stages in the child's development in art:

1. Scribbling (2 to 3 years).
2. Line (4 years).
3. Descriptive Symbolism (5 to 6 years).
4. Realism (7 to 9 years).
5. Visual Realism (10 to 11 years).
6. Repression (11 to 14 years).
7. Artistic Revival (experienced by some).

His stages indicate a gradual growing from pure motor activity to linear storytelling. Realistic tendencies are then initiated in the transition to older childhood with the discovery of spatial depth and motion. The general tendency is for repression and a discarding of art in the early adolescent years. Many may enter such repression at an earlier age if they are not provided with adequate encouragement and guidance. A few children experience confidence leading to art involvement and further development of their capabilities in mid and late adolescence.

Viktor Lowenfeld published *Creative and Mental Growth* in 1947, and in its content six stages of development are described. His work draws from much of the earlier research and theory but has had the advantage of placing the material in a manner that has received very popular acceptance in this country. He describes the following stages:

1. Scribbling (2 to 4 years)—Experiences of Body Motion.
   Disordered Substage—Lack of Motor Control (to 18 mo.).
   Longitudinal Substage—Visual-Motor Control (18 mo. to 2 years).
   Circular Substage—Experimentation with Visual-Motor Control (2 to 3 years).
   Naming Substage—Change from kinesthetic activity to Mental Activity (3 to 4 years).
2. Pre-Schematic (4 to 7 years)—Searching for Representational Symbols.
3. Schematic (7 to 9 years)—Storytelling By Using and Repeating Form, Space, and Color Schema. (The experience is expressed in Form by Exaggerations, Omissions, and Distortions. It is expressed in Space by Foldover, X-Ray, and Moving-Time Sequence Views.)
4. Dawning Realism (9 to 11 years)— Spatial Depth expresses deeper social awareness in the "Gang Age."
5. Pseudo-Realism (11 to 13 years)—Critical Awareness from Physical Change Stifles Many in "Early Adolescence."
6. Period of Decision (Adolescence).

From 1920 on, other disciplines began to take great interest in the child's art. McCarty used H-T-P drawings of children in 1924 to establish relationships between drawing characteristics and intelligence. In 1926 Goodenough published the Draw-a-Man Test which very accurately assesses intelligence through details in the child's drawing of a man. In 1963 Harris published an extensive revision of the Goodenough scale which holds broader implications for general intellectual maturity, or what he terms "conceptual maturity."

By 1930 psychologists were becoming primarily involved with the child's art as a core area for studying perception. Many were either strongly influenced by Gestalt psychology or even built their entire theory of child art from that reference. Most notable among these were Bender, Read, Schaefer-Simmern, and Arnheim.

There were several who stimulated an interest in perception. Hartlaub in 1922 and Jaensch in 1923 both wrote of "eidetic" gifts which were defined as mental pictures produced as an intermediary image between mental function and the act of perception. The theory was popular for a time but is essentially one more rationalization structured to compare the child to the paleolithic cave artist. Some of Jaensch's observations were the basis for gestalt experimentation.

While Britsch was not directly involved with the Gestalt School, his theories tie in very well with their principles. In 1926 he recognized that form develops from simple character in early childhood to more complex character with maturity and that the greatest directionality (vertical vs. horizontal) in the early years gradually changes to subtle variations of angle. He especially noted the matter of figure-ground relationship and the child's natural feeling for organization on the drawing surface. The influence of his work was introduced into this country by Henry Schaefer-Simmern (1948) who in turn highly influenced the work of Arnheim (1954) and Kellogg (1955). The terms used by these writers are often confusing, as they appear to be self-contradictory (*ex.:* visual conception). They basically aim, it seems, at revealing how the child develops a feeling of form, first from motor activity and then in conjunction with visual perception. The emphasis of the gestaltist, therefore, is basically a consideration of development from a view of the cognitive factor in sensory perception.

The earliest or more "primitive" activity of the child is motor activity, and the loop or whorl is the initial form of this expression in art. Seeman (1934) and Mira (1940) support this view. Bender (1944) mentions the gestalt form factor in the child in a very thorough manner. She states, "Motor activity develops first or at least independently of the optic imagery." She further clarifies the gestalt view by stating:

> Gestalt psychology holds that the whole or total quality of the image is perceived. . . . The perceptual experience is a gestalt or configuration or pattern in which the whole is more than the sum of the parts. Organized units or structuralized configurations are the primary form of biological reactions . . . the organism in the act of perception always adds something new to the experienced perception. . . . The final gestalt is the result of the original pattern in space (visual pattern), the temporal factor of becoming, and the personal sensori-motor factor.[1]

Her Visual-Motor Gestalt Test is perhaps her greatest contribution from this premise and is a means of recognizing the individual's capability to experience and organize self in the space and time of material reality. The test is structured in regard to perceiving motion characteristics in directionality, proximity, balance, closure, and other gestalt principles.

Read (1945) stresses the aesthetic factor from the gestalt viewpoint, a factor of strong agreement found later in the writings of both Arnheim and Kellogg. He quotes Koffka, one of the leaders of the Gestalt School:

> "Perception tends toward balance and symmetry; or differently expressed: balance and symmetry are perceptual characteristics of the visual world which will be realized whenever the external conditions allow it."[2]

Read further states:

> If these facts are true—and the experiments of the Gestalt psychologists leave little doubt about the matter—then it is quite legitimate to call this factor of 'feeling' in perception and other processes, *aesthetic*. . . . Balance and symmetry, proportion and rhythm, are basic factors in experience: indeed, they are the only elements by means of which experience can be organized into persisting patterns, and it is of their nature that they imply grace, economy and efficiency. What works right; and the result, for the individual, is that heightening of the senses which is aesthetic enjoyment.[3]

Such enjoyment is obviously what the child seeks to naturally develop and enjoy. It implies a homeostasis or wholeness when achieved. It is easily recognized why Read is so open to accepting the gestalt principles for aesthetics when we also see how accepting he is of the Jungian psychoanalytic viewpoint. It, too, deals with this same unity or wholeness through the mandala form.

We could say that Read is as much, or more, Jungian as he is gestaltist, and through relating the *introvert* and *extrovert* concepts of Carl Jung to the four "directions" of the mandala, he arrives at eight types or categories of art:

1. Lauretta Bender, *Child Psychiatric Techniques,* pp. 50-51.
2. Read, *Education Through Art,* p. 60.
3. Ibid., pp. 60-61.

1. Enumerative   (Extrovert-Thinking Type)
2. Organic   (Introvert-Thinking Type)
3. Decorative   (Extrovert-Feeling Type)
4. Imaginative   (Introvert-Feeling Type)
5. Rhythmical Pattern   (Extrovert-Intuitive Type)
6. Structural Form   (Introvert-Intuitive Type)
7. Empathetic   (Extrovert-Sensation Type)
8. Expressionist   (Introvert-Sensation Type)

Lowenfeld (1939) spoke of two perceptual types: the *visual* and the *haptic*. The visual type is stated to regard a person who identifies basically from visual environmental experiences. He could be recognized to be visually dependent, for maintaining self-identification, upon his environment and is essentially what Jung calls an extrovert. The haptic type is primarily concerned with his own bodily sensations and with the tactual space about himself. He is essentially what Jung labels an introvert. We must be careful to note that Lowenfeld sees these types on a continuum and not as discrete classifications. Most people, therefore, have both attributes to some degree but will tend to fit more into one category than the other. Many writers have grossly misinterpreted Lowenfeld on this point. Generally the visual type will follow these characteristics:

1. Through his art he will indicate a need to bring the world close to himself.
2. He will be biased toward analytical process.
3. His art will be spectator-oriented.
4. He will attempt to indicate spatial depth in his two-dimensional art and thereby reveal his social dependency.
5. He will attempt to draw realistically by suggesting light and shadow characteristics along with motion in his art.
6. He will use color according to realistic appearance.
7. He will tend to lack sensitivity for tactual factors.
8. His linear drawing will tend to be of a broken or "sketchy" character.

The haptic type artist will produce according to the following:

1. Through his art he reveals a concern for projecting his inner world or identification.
2. He will be biased toward synthetic process.
3. His art will be participant-oriented in that he will place himself as identifying from the center of the drawing space.
4. His two-dimensional art will have a flat and decorative appearance.
5. He will produce from an emotional identification with his subject and exaggerate, omit, and distort form according to emotional significance.
6. He will use color in a subjective or symbolic sense.
7. He will express a sensitivity for tactual and kinesthetic involvement.
8. His linear means will be bold and continuous in character.

Lowenfeld noted that the younger child consistently expresses in a haptic manner but that with progressing age the majority of individuals reveal a tendency for visual aptitude.

Witkin (1954) found two perceptual types which he called *field-dependent* and *field-independent*. Recent study indicates that there is a relationship between Lowenfeld's visual type and Witkin's field-dependent type—both are extroverted or dependent visually toward their environment and lack a sensitivity or respect for bodily cues in space. Witkin found that the parent who dominates the child produces a dependency by "constricting" the child's growth. In similar manner a relationship exists between Lowenfeld's haptic type and

Witkin's field-independent type. Both are sensitive to bodily positioning and weight and esteem the body generally more than their countertypes. The "growth-fostering" parent was primarily responsible for this identification according to Witkin.

Piaget (1950) has been very influential in clarifying the development of the child by a discussion of three general stages:

1. Sensorimotor Period (to 2 years).
2. Concrete Operations (2 to 11 years).
     Pre-Operational Substage (2 to 4 years).
     Intuitive Thought Substage (4 to 7 years).
     Concrete Operations Substage (7 to 11 years).
3. Formal Operations Period (11 to 15 years).

His stages deal primarily with the perception of space, though the factor of time is also strongly considered. Like the gestaltist, he sees visualized forms as arriving through early motor play. His Pre-Operational Substage is very similar to Lowenfeld's "naming" period in scribbling, and they cover the same period of development. At that time the child is labeling the object, but there is little connection which would allow identification in the context of form or space. The Intuitive Thought Substage is similar to Lowenfeld's Pre-Schematic Stage in which the child is attempting to develop a schema and organize space. The Concrete Operations Substage is similar to Lowenfeld's Schematic Stage, but Piaget places emphasis upon the conceptualization of spatial perceptions and time sequences which indicate that the child feels a real part of his environment.

Tarmo Pasto (1965), another recent writer, deals very extensively with the physical and emotional identification of the child in his environment in the early years. Pasto traces the emotional-motor experience of the young child in clarifying his "Space-Frame" theory. In his discussion he deals with a Jungian reference of symbolism in form and wonderfully relates it, from a gestalt influence, to the motor development of the child. While he does not actually label stages, they are described and are approximately as follows:

1. Swing Scribble (12 to 18 mo.)—"The joy of sound and the feel of muscle" —sensorimotor experiencing.
2. The Circle (2 to 3 years)—"The creative, the mother image, the feminine self"—suggests the child bound up emotionally in the mother but is seeking to be a physical entity as well.
3. The Cross (3 to 4 years)—"Oppositional, the problem of the masculine and the feminine"—the paradox of a sexual role clarified.
4. The Rectangle (4 years)—Indicating closure of the ego—the inner resolving of identity in the environment.
5. The Homunculus (5 years)—The inner reality faces the outer reality.
6. Reality (6 to 10 years)—The exterior concept formed and the child moves into the perceptual-motor space-frame.
7. Deterioration (11 years on)—Tendency to visual appearance and loss of motor identity in reality.

The symbolical aspects of form in Pasto's theory are extremely important for our later consideration of the child and psychopathology.

Indebtedness is recognized for all of the mentioned basic theoretical constructs, as well as to the many writers who have aided in their promulgation. With this body of reference in mind, it is now intended that we should turn our attention to the typical development of the child to note basic factors of significance for our discussion of the exceptional child.

Significance of Drawing Forms in Early Childhood

If a child is given a crayon before he is eighteen months of age, he will probably put it in his mouth and suck on it. After a while he may manipulate it by waving his arm, and he may even randomly hit at a paper. In such a case we would obtain what Lowenfeld called a disordered scribble (fig. 9.)

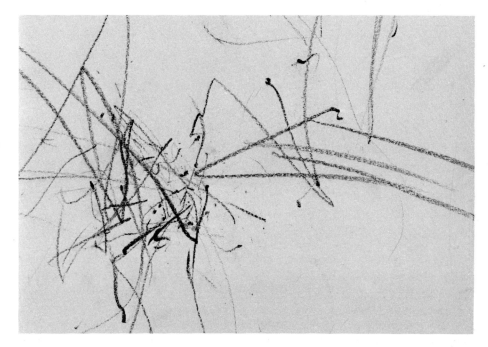

Figure 9. Disordered Scribble by Debbie, 16 months.

Such a drawing would indicate a lack of visual-motor control and would hold little significance beyond that fact. By eighteen months to two years the child gains control of the visual-motor factor and begins drawing a longitudinal or swinging-arc scribble. In figure 10 we can almost see spilled milk in the tray of the high chair being slopped by a small arm which moves back and forth. At this age the child is into everything—tearing paper, tipping things over, open-

Figure 10. Swing Scribble by Debbie, 18 months.

ing drawers and strewing the contents on the floor, pulling off buttons, and, in short, getting a sensory joy out of anything and everything. In this sensori-motor period he is testing reality and learning about form through manipulative and visual activity. It is one of the most creative periods in life, and we must not hamper his investigation. It will be well if we prepare the scene by providing an area with numerous and acceptable objects and materials. Plastic pans, string, balls, blocks of wood, and cardboard boxes are only a few of the many wonderful things from which the child may experience.

At about two years of age his scribbling begins to move in a circular motion (fig. 11), and if he has been rolling out coils with clay, he will now begin to roll balls from the same material. The circular form is the earliest form and holds great significance. The circle is the simplest gestalt form. The edges are

Figure 11. Circular Scribble by Debbie, 2 years.

composed of points equally distant from the center, and thus our attention is usually drawn to the centrality of the circle. Symbolically the "centeredness" implies self as well as dependency. Certainly the child of two begins to stress himself as a self-entity. It seems that all we must do is say "yes" and he will say "no!" We call him and he runs the other way. But the child, while seeking to be a physical entity, is very much bound up emotionally with the mother. The circle is a primary feminine form.

What we have just stated has set the stage for what we all know to be true —two-year-olds are impossible people! We even speak of the "terrible twos." The child is in a tremendous paradox. He wants to be physically independent but remains emotionally dependent. Just watch him get frustrated at trying to button his shirt and then try to help him! That will almost always boil him over. But a few minutes later he may cling to mother when something has frightened him. We must encourage him to be physically independent and at the same time provide the reassurance of emotional security.

By two and a half the child may burst out of his tight circle and recognize other self-entities. In figure 12 we may observe such an expression in what Pasto calls a "burst into life."

Now let us carefully note how important it is that the child feels the love of the parent at two years. Unless the child is accepted and fulfilled by the parent, he will continue to seek that basis of identity. It is also important to emphasize that the parent must encourage him to stand on his own feet and be independent. One of the greatest problems of our day is parents who absorb the personality of their children and thus fulfill their own need for affection in the child rather than in each other.

We begin to note a dramatic departure from the circular form when the child is around three years of age. He discovers the vertical line. At first he will repeat it over and over as if it were a new toy. Often, as in figure 13, it

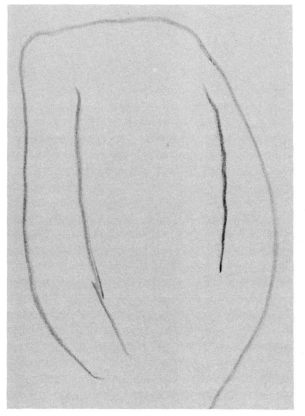

above: **Figure 12.** "Feeding the Ducks" by Debbie, 2 1/2 years.

left: **Figure 13.** "I and My Bear on the Bed" by Debbie, 3 years 2 months.

will appear in conjunction with the circle. The vertical line is rather obviously the first symbol for a man (figs. 14 and 15). One of the most interesting records of a child that a parent may collect is that child's figure concept from the first vertical line to the full, detailed figure (figs. 16-19).

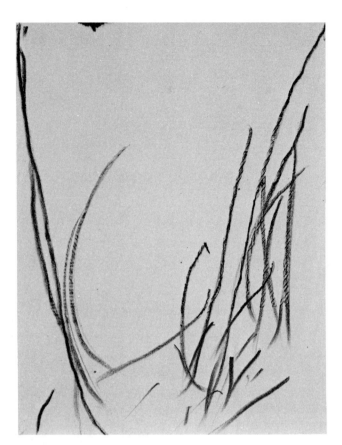

left: **Figure 14.** Debbie, 2 years 10 months.

below: **Figure 15.** "Man" by Debbie, 3 years.

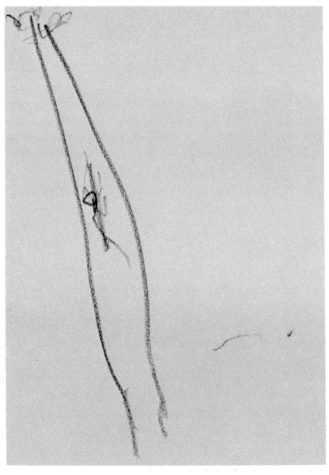

Figure 16. "Man" by Sara, 45 months

Figure 17. "Man" by Sara, 50 months

Figure 18. "With Mother" by Sara, 59 months

Figure 19. "Self" by Sara, 63 months

Figure 20.   Oppositional Lines by Debbie, 3 years 1 month

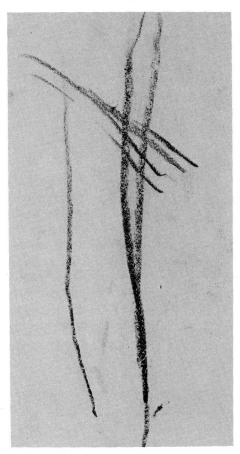

Figure 21.   Cross Form by Debbie, 3 years 1 month.

The strong paradoxical dilemma of the child who is three and a half is revealed by the vertical-horizontal line drawings of the child. Symbolically the vertical is masculine, and the horizontal now represents the feminine principle. The child between three and four years is attempting to work out a sex-role identification. His models are the parents, and it is important that they play their roles well. Father goes to work and mother takes care of the house, and so on. If the child does not resolve the self-sexual role at this age, the paradox will continue and perhaps never be resolved. It is little wonder that the great medical centers of today find it more advantageous to change the sexual characteristics of the body than to change the personality. We can expect a typical three-year-old to be a bit paranoid, for he is in opposition within himself (fig. 20). The oppositional lines form what is best labeled the *cross* (fig. 21). This form usually speaks of such a paradoxical dilemma. The threat that lies within, however, is usually projected in such a manner that it appears to be from without, and the attitude of the child will therefore be something like, "I am better than you!"

At four years the child discovers the rectangle. Four is the number of man, and the simple rectangle quickly turns into what Pasto calls the "grid." This structured form suggests a pigeonholing, and that is essentially its symbolic significance—putting everything in its place. The child, in order to close the ego, must see himself in the context of his environment, and he therefore organizes his environment.

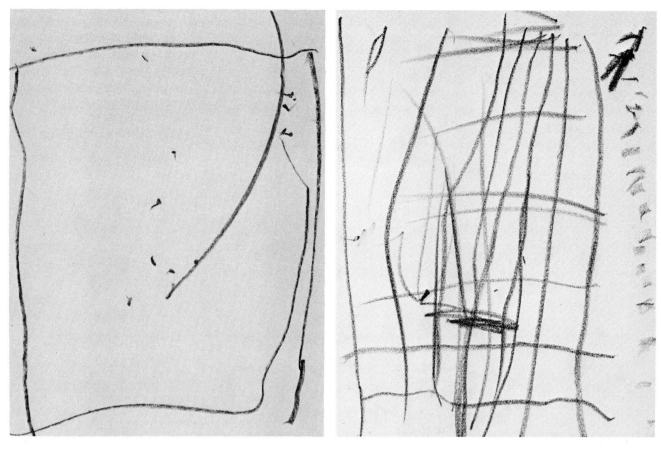

Figure 22. "New Blue Car" by Debbie, 3 years 5 months   **Figure 23.** Grid Form by Debbie, 3 years 9 months

At four or four and a half he will ask questions. They may appear to be obvious questions to the adult and therefore "stupid." For example, the child may ask, "Is the sun going to come up tomorrow?" or "How long is an hour?" Essentially the child is asking the parent to "tell him how it is" and thus reinforce his view of reality. The child may then try to put the parent in his place according to his own wishes. Through such behavior he is actually asking for discipline which will again reinforce an idea of proper relationship and authority. Discipline, if properly administered, will always lead to greater security and self-discipline. Our society today suffers from ego-weak individuals who have always found the walls and edges of their parents and society to be easily moved. Have you ever wondered why a child likes to play in a box? It has walls which provide a physical security. We all need walls and edges of a physical or psychological type to reinforce our emotional security. At this age it will be of benefit to the child if drastic changes in the home and family are not made. Moving every few months and broken homes create a turmoil and insecurity within a child which can never be properly and fully assessed. We must bear in mind that security must come from within if we are to find a healthy and creative personality which will function to the utmost of its capacity. When security is not found within, we will evidence an obsessive-compulsive "organizer" who must constantly "put things where they belong" in order to feel secure. This may be manifested in many ways, and all we need note here is that we certainly are living in a hyperorganizational society; a nation of "joiners."

As the child moves from a pure kinesthetic activity to a conceptual activity, we begin to have the expression of many small tales. The child is becoming what Levenstein appropriately called a "storyteller." In some cases the mental concepts of the story will be verbally expressed along with the drawing, and the drawing may or may not reveal the detailed meaning (fig. 24). At other times, there may be almost full recognition of subject as the child moves into a search for representational symbols which will suffice to express his concepts. The child is now in Lowenfeld's pre-schematic stage.

Figure 24. A Story Drawing by Debbie, 4 years

If we consider the total development of the child up to four and a half to five years, we realize the tremendous tasks which he has encountered and has attempted to surmount. He has sought to see himself as an entity apart from his mother, he has attempted to resolve a self-sex role, and he has begun to form ego-closure by identifying with self in respect to a large and often confusing real environment. If he has been to some degree successful in these tasks, we may expect him to express drawings which indicate such a "wholeness" or "unification." A mandala-like figure or form is often just such a form, and it may be drawn as a total abstraction, or it may be linked to a subject concept. At this point we may truly say that the child has entered the "golden age" of his art expression.

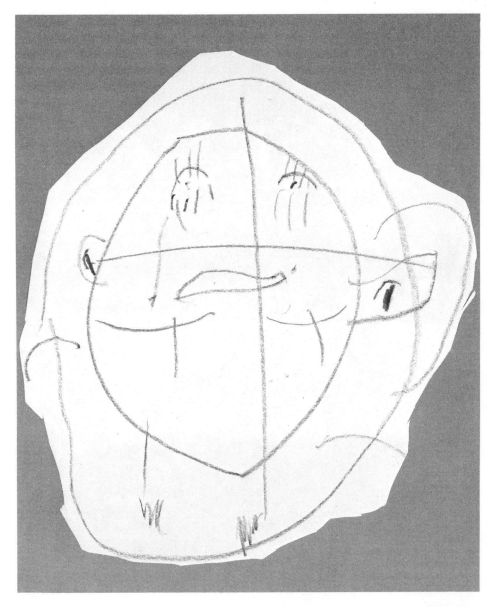

Figure 25.   "Humpty-Dumpty. He Is Crying" by Debbie, 5 years. (Notice the mandala-like quality.)

Aesthetic Quality and Spatial Organization

Between five and six years of age, a wonderful gestalt organization of space accounts for high aesthetic quality in the child's art expression. As the child begins to richly describe experiences through his continuously developing form concepts, he also moves ahead in recognizing his position in respect to the world about himself. In figures 26 and 27 we note the emotional relationship of the self to another object or person. We must note here that the earliest spatial relationships are therefore physically and emotionally significant. The child expresses in regard to what is his own or what he may want and will then organize the space around the immediate self-image upon that basis.

Figure 26. "Debbie Running After Sara to Hurt Her" by Debbie, 5 years 2 months. (Note: Debbie's self-image has large hands—they are significant to inflict harm. Sara's body is composed of just a "body" with legs—they are necessary for running.)

Figure 27. "I Am Playing with My Blocks" by child 5 years

As the child's world opens to new possibilities of meaningful relationships, he begins to structure and organize more fully. His games may be excellent examples of this desire because they are of a spontaneous and natural character (fig. 28).

Figure 28.   A driveway chalk game, 5 years

While the child at four was seeking to be told "how things are," he now may become indignant at times and attempt to force his own will upon others. He will be preoccupied with the rectangle as an expression of putting everything, including people, in place. The parent may experience the child's sassing him and calling him names. Such behavior should meet with firm resistance in order to provide the child with the security of reinforced relationship which he is ultimately seeking. Such a "game" may prove puzzling and disturbing to the naïve parent. The parent who "plays the game" well will learn to accept the child's behavior in terms regarding the underlying need and not be unduly ruffled by the outer show of insolence. It is natural that such outbursts and difficulty will appear in greatest strength when traveling, entertaining, or otherwise out of the normal routine.

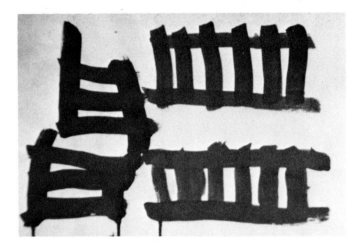

Figure 29. "Boxes." Tempera painting by child 5 years.

Figure 30. "My Brother Is in the Crib" by child 5 years. (He has been organized—put in his box or place—where he belongs.)

By five and a half to six years the child will begin to "fit in" and become a cooperating member of society. He will, in short, learn to "give" as well as "take." This will be expressed in his art by a baseline upon which objects finally settle. In every respect it relates to the child's taking an active social part in the space-time (motion) world.

Figure 31. "I Am Riding My Bike" by boy 5 years.

Figure 32. A 5-year-old's painting depicting a schematic space. (Note the umbilical tie to the house, which symbolizes the mother.)

Through this "golden age" it is very evident that the total organization of the child to his environment is reflected in his harmonious distribution and handling of line, form, and color on the surface of his drawing or painting. He is a naïve and natural artist, for it is from such a source that true art is expressed. Very often the older exceptional person who continues to grapple with these same early needs will express in the same wonderful manner.

left: **Figure 33.** Tempera painting by child 5 years. (High aesthetic quality.)

below: **Figure 34.** "Myself" by Sara, 5 years.

opposite: **Figure 35.** "A Mexican Red-Riding Hood Spilling Chili Beans on the Way to Grandmother's House" by boy 8 years.

Schematic Storytelling

By seven years the physical-emotional motor-space experience, which was responsible for high aesthetic products, is now subjugated to rational and social forces in the development of the child. Verworn stressed the rational factor in his term *ideoplastic,* and Piaget regards the same force through his term *concrete-operations.* The child has now arrived at a full nonverbal concept language, or *schema,* which encompasses form and space. The *idea* of things becomes predominant, and while he has not by any means lost his motor-space feeling, his principal efforts are directed at storytelling. His art, as observed by Burt, is essentially *descriptive symbolism.*

The story may be called linear at first as the child treats space-time by moving from left to right along a baseline. Such a linear storytelling ability is one of the best tests of reading readiness, for he is indicating now a capacity for identifying symbols moving on a common line from left to right. It is interesting to note that Lowenfeld finds the origin of the baseline to be kinesthetic. How important the physiological-emotional identification is in providing a foundation for rational development and expression! Most appropriate literature in early childhood, such as Mother Goose, will have a strong rhythmical, and thus physical, basis.

The linear storytelling may be puzzling at times because of its basic conceptual characters. In figure 36 we note two people eating lunch together at a round table. The table itself serves as the baseline. To understand the drawing as the child conceived of it, we must consider the figures and table cut from the paper and the figures folded down at the point where their wrists touch the table. Then the figures will "sit up" to the table. Lowenfeld calls this a "fold-over" view and considers it a deviation from the child's normal schematic space.

In figure 37 we note a similar fold-over view as a man drives his car to the toll station and pays his fee. The car itself, in this case, is folded up on end. The inside of the toll booth was extremely significant to the child so he left the exterior wall off. Lowenfeld calls this type of space deviation an "x-ray" view.

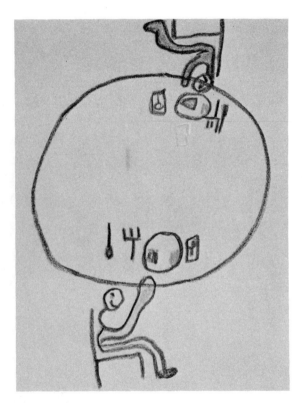

Figure 36. "Eating Lunch" by boy 7 years

Figure 37. "At the Toll Station" by boy 8 years

Through the schematic period we often notice how successful the child is in essentially and vividly telling a story. In figures 38-41 we find various children responding to the familiar episode of Jonah. Each child seemed to find a different portion of the experience especially important as he identified with Jonah. An interesting x-ray view was drawn of Jonah asleep in the hold of the ship. In another child's drawing, Jonah is thrown overboard during the storm into the mouth of the waiting whale. A third child drew an x-ray view of Jonah all tangled up in seaweed inside the whale. The whale finally spits him out on dry land after he decides to obey God and go preach at Ninevah.

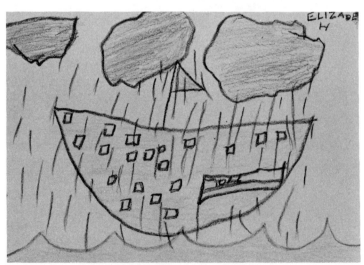

Figure 38. "Jonah in the Ship"

Figure 39. "Jonah Thrown to the Whale"

Figure 40. "Jonah in the Whale"

Figure 41. "Jonah Spit Out"

As a rule the child may be sensitized best, at this age, by story motivation that tends to recall vivid imagery. Such stimulation may be attributed to the initial efforts of Cizek. Many children do, of course, have powerful experiences which highly motivate them for drawing in a "spontaneous" manner. In figure 42 we find a good example of such a circumstance. The girl came home from school and mother simply asked her how things were at school. She said the teacher got mad and yelled at the kids and stamped her feet. After gesturing a few minutes, she got her crayons out and drew the picture of her teacher. This drawing reveals the impact we may have on a child who identifies emotionally with us—perhaps when we are the least aware of our influence. This same teacher, who motivated art without knowing it, may be a poor stimulator of art when she consciously directs her efforts to that end. This should emphasize to us

right: **Figure 42.** "Teacher Got Mad" by girl 8 years

below: **Figure 43.** "You Take My Picture and I'll Take Yours." Construction by boy 8 years.

that children need teachers who are themselves flexible and who can act out emotionally. This teacher, of course, was *not* acting.

Because the child begins to become set in his ideological processes, he must be provided with material experiences which will reactivate and encourage flexible exploration and inventiveness. In figure 43 we see just one result from a group experience with scrap materials. The class was simply given towel tubes, egg cartons, boxes, string, and tape, and the children were encouraged to "make something" after they had been sensitized to the characteristics of the materials.

Social Self-Concept of the Older Child

An increased awareness of self in the social environment becomes very evident with many children by nine years of age. This will be especially true for the extroverted child whom Lowenfeld calls *visually oriented* and Witkin labels *field-dependent*. The spatial depth factor will be evidence of such a perceptual tendency, and a type of realism will begin to appear in the art product. A use of "meaningful surface" between baselines and a relative positioning used in conjunction with it will often be the early suggestions of this visual-social dependency (fig. 44). In a short time some individuals will draw with a strong

Figure 44.   Drawing by girl 9 years

illusion of spatial depth through the surface plane, relative positioning, relative size, overlapping, and atmospheric effects (fig. 45).

The introverted child, whom Lowenfeld calls *haptic,* will retain a flat, decorative quality in the drawing product, and there will be a very apparent lack of motion (fig. 46). Such a child would be labeled "field-independent" by Witkin.

Figure 45. "Kite Flying" by girl 10 years.

Figure 46. "Kite Flying" by girl 10 years.

Along with the spatial factors which reveal social-perceptual orientation, we now note a growing stress on sexual identification in the human figure drawings. The gang development of this age is based upon such an identity. In figure 47 we see a typical stress on the hair as a virility symbol, and this emphasis will be noticed among both sexes. Details, in short, are added as social-emotional factors of sexual identification at this age. The human figure, from a stress upon such identity, can be expected to be highly distorted and even bizarre among the boys (fig. 48) or highly idealized and glamorous among the girls (fig. 49).

It is important to encourage the drawing of the human figure as the individual moves in and through adolescence, for it will offer the opportunity for the resolv-

right: **Figure 47.** "Playing Ball" by boy 11 years. (Notice the visual factor of motion in crease behind knees.)

below: **Figure 48.** Self-image of boy 12 years

below right: **Figure 49.** Self-image of girl 11 years

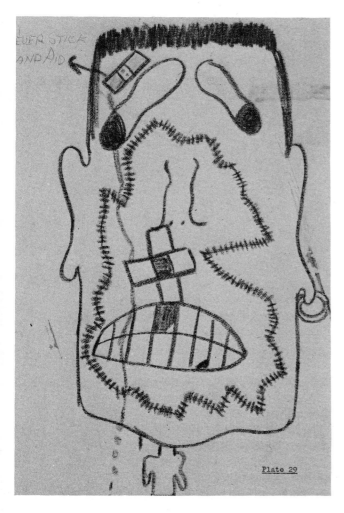

ing of discrepancy between the sexual-ideal and the acceptance of the sexual self. Physical growth and development in adolescence literally force a new body-image and destroy that which we have known to be a child.

Summary

From infancy to early adolescence the child passes through several basic phases of development as reflected in art. Earliest material experiencing is of a sensorimotor character; and through the manipulation and visual experimentation of this period, an ability to produce forms is achieved. While these forms may be easily recognized as evolving from a simple to complex character, in a visual-motor gestalt sense, they also represent symbolically the life tasks of the young child. The circle indicates symbolically the child identifying as a physical entity apart from the mother and yet being bound up in emotional dependence with her person. The cross form suggests the sexual paradox of the child in his attempt to identify through the parental roles. The rectangle suggests the ego-closure of the child as he attempts to clarify self in the context of his environment.

By six years of age the child begins to settle into the real world and become a social part of its interrelationships. He previously has accumulated details in his drawing as he grew, and they reflect his intellectual growth, but now he arrives at a full rational reference of schematic form and space by seven years of age. The rich aesthetic quality of his physical-emotional reference in the early years is now subordinated to ideological storytelling. Perceptual types become evident in the art of the nine-year-old child as he matures socially.

The child will be a social-perceptual extrovert and thus visual and field-dependent in his art, or he will be a social-perceptual introvert and be haptic and field-independent in his art. He will in either case, and to some degree, be gang-oriented from a need to identify more deeply with a self-sexual role. Such identification will lead the boy to exaggerate in bizarre images of self-projection, while the girl will tend to idealize herself in the image of a glamorous, mature female.

References

ARNHEIM, RUDOLF. *Art and Visual Perception.* Berkeley, Calif.: University of California Press, 1954.

BALDWIN, JOHN. *Die Entwicklung des Geistes Beim Kinde und bei der rasse.* Berlin, 1898.

BARNES, EARL. "A Study of Children's Drawings." *Pedagogical Sem.* 2 (1893): 451-463.

BENDER, LAURETTA. *Child Psychiatric Techniques.* Springfield, Ill.: Charles C Thomas, Publisher, 1952.

BRITSCH, GUSTAF. *Theorie der Bildenden Kunst.* Munich: F. Bruckmann, 1926.

BURT, CYRIL. *Mental and Scholastic Tests.* London: P. S. King and Son, 1921.

CLARK, ARTHUR. "The Children's Attitudes Toward Perspective Problems." *University of California Studies in Education 1* (1902): 283-294.

GOODENOUGH, FLORENCE. *Measurement of Intelligence by Drawings.* New York: Harcourt, Brace and World, 1926.

HARRIS, DALE. *Children's Drawings as Measures of Intellectual Maturity.* New York: Harcourt, Brace and World, 1963.

HARTLAUB, G. F. *Das Genius im Kinde.* Breslau, 1922.

JAENSCH, E. R. *Uber den Aufbau der Wahrnehmungswelt und Ihre Struktur im Jugendalter.* Leipzig, 1923.

KELLOGG, RHODA. *What Children Scribble and Why.* San Francisco: Golden Gate Nursery School, 1955.

LEVENSTEIN, SIGFRIED. "Kinderzeichnungen biz Zum 14ten." *Lebensjahr.* Leipzig, 1904.

LICHTWARK, ALFRED. *Die Kunst in der Schule,* 1887.

LOWENFELD, VIKTOR. *The Nature of Creative Activity.* London: Routledge and Kegan Paul, Ltd., 1939.

——— *Creative and Mental Growth.* New York: The Macmillan Co., 1947.

LUKENS, HERMAN. "A Study of Children's Drawings in the Early Years." *Pedagogical Sem. 4* (1894): 79-110.

McCARTY, STELLA. *Children's Drawings.* Baltimore: Williams and Wilkins, 1924.

MAITLAND, LOUISE. "What Children Draw to Please Themselves." *Inland Educator, 1*:87.

MIRA, E. "Myokinetic Psychodiagnosis: A New Technique for Exploring the Connotative Trends of Personality." *Proceedings of the Royal Society of Medicine 33* (1940): 173-194.

PASTO, TARMO. *The Space-Frame Experience in Art.* New York: A. S. Barnes and Co., Inc., 1965.

PIAGET, JEAN. *The Psychology of Intelligence.* London: Routledge and Kegan Paul, Ltd., 1950.

READ, HERBERT. *Education through Art.* New York: Pantheon Books, 1958.

RICCI, CORRADO. "L'art de Bambini. Bologna, 1887, Leipzig, 1906. *Pedagogical Sem. 3* (1894); 302-307.

SCHAEFER-SIMMERN. *The Unfolding of Artistic Activity.* Berkeley, Calif.: University of Calfornia Press, 1948.

SEEMAN, ERNEST. "Development of the Pictoral Aptitude in Children." *Character and Personality 2* (1934): 209-221.

STERN, WILLIAM. "Spezielle Beschreibung der Ausstellung Freier Kinderzeichnunger aus Breslau." *Bericht Über den Kongress fur Kinderforschung.* Berlin, 1908.

SULLY, JAMES. *Studies of Childhood.* New York: D. Appleton and Co., 1895.

VERWORN, MAX. "Kinderkunst und Urgeschichte," *Korrespondenz der Deutscher Anthropologische Gesellschaft 27* (1907): 42-46.

VIOLA, WILHELM. *Child Art.* Peoria, Ill.: Chas. Bennett Co., 1944.

WITKIN, HERMAN; LEWIS, H. B.; HERTZMAN, M.; MACHOVER, K.; MEISSNER, P. BRETNALL; and WAPNER, S. *Personality Through Perception: An Experimental and Clinical Study.* New York: Harper and Brothers, 1954.

PART TWO Art for the Exceptional Child

The Mentally
Deficient Personality in Art 3

Many children in our society are labeled "retarded" because their intelligence quotient is demonstrated to be somewhat below average. About one of every four of these children is found to suffer cerebral dysfunction and therefore may be properly labeled "neurologically handicapped." The larger number of children is often greatly difficult to diagnose and label in a specific etiological classification. Close examination will reveal that this sizable group is composed of individuals who often are not mentally deficient but who are, rather, essentially deprived or disturbed. It is important to recognize the fact that mental *function* may be highly impaired by many factors other than low mental *capability*. Our intent in this section is to discuss a relatively small group of those labeled retarded; those whom we will recognize to have mental deficiency as a basic impairment.

We will note the common labels and classifications for the exceptional child who is mentally deficient and then turn our attention to the behavioral manifestations which more appropriately describe him to us. Finally, we will note the teaching-therapy process in art for this type child and the character of material experiences which generally will be of most value in promoting his growth.

Definition and Classification of Mental Deficiency

Being a nation of "label makers" we have called the mentally deficient individual by such terms as *feebleminded, subnormal, mentally handicapped,* and *inferior*. We have noted that he is behaviorally "slow" or "backward." Some, in attempting a more clinical description, have used the term *endogenous* for the mentally deficient child to suggest a *familial* or *hereditary* etiology and thereby set him apart from that which is *exogenous* and implies brain injury. Such a classification, of course, is weak in that many children, as in Down's syndrome cases, may or may not suffer their weakened rational power from the hereditary contribution of the parents. In Down's syndrome, commonly known as mongolism, recent research has indicated that a simple physical "accident" or failure in the chromosome attachments is often responsible for the abnormality. The hereditary characteristics in such a situation are normal. This becomes important to consider when we especially note the number of children with Down's syndrome—about one in every 600 to 700 births.

It seems logical that, in the end, all considerations point to assessment of mental deficiency on the sole basis of intellectual functioning *with the strong provision that study must indicate that the child's general physical and emotional environment and potential are found to be reasonably normal in all other respects. If this is not the case, then such a diagnosis should always be pronounced with the most careful qualifications.* In the early years, before adequate rational assessment may be made, much information can be gained by observation of the physical-emotional responses of behavior. A few key questions are—

1. Did the child develop an awareness of the mother's face by four to six weeks?

2. At six weeks was the child able to hold his head up for a few seconds when held horizontally on his stomach?
3. Was he attentive to objects and sounds at three months?
4. Had he stopped drooling at one year?
5. How old was he when he first rolled over? Sat up? Stood?
6. Was he able to walk at two years of age?
7. Did he speak in short sentences at three years?

By the time the child is five years of age, proper assessment of functioning intelligence may be made if mental deficiency is suspected. Such evaluation will ordinarily be the chief basis for school placement. In the past it has been popular to classify the child according to *educable* (IQ 50-75) and *trainable* (IQ below 50) levels, but the National Association for Retarded Children and the American Association on Mental Deficiency are now encouraging the following for general use:

1. Mildly Retarded   IQ of 70-85
2. Moderately Retarded IQ of 50-70
3. Severely Retarded   IQ below 50

These classifications for children with no brain injury, or other recognized organic basis of impairment, were earlier proposed by a committee of the American Psychiatric Association.

For our purposes it must be emphasized here that our consideration of mental deficiency will involve below-average mental functioning assumed to be caused by a weak brain capability. From such impairment the child is not provided with the ability to structure and maintain a normal life function in the material world. That such an impairment will, with time, tend to secondarily affect the individual's physical, emotional, and social functioning is understandable also.

Mentally Deficient Art Expression

The reality structuring of the mentally deficient child may be compared to a water pipe with a valve on the faucet. The pipe or body operates sufficiently except for the valve which here represents the brain. The valve allows the good, pure water of experience to flow through but never at an adequate rate to properly feed the mind. Insufficient communication of the life stream of experience leaves the mind unable to successfully structure the reality we would anticipate, and this lack will be evidenced in all behavior. It is suspected that only at the point when the personality leaves the limitation of the body will a greater or perfect reality be found. In the meantime, it is our opportunity to minister to the needs of the individual and encourage the unfolding of that potential which lies within.

The H-T-P drawings of mentally deficient children generally reveal simple form concepts produced with good motor coordination. The specific intelligence of the child may readily be assessed, according to its function, by use of the Goodenough Scale. A general guess by an experienced observer, however, will often come close enough for general practical purposes. In figures 50 and 51 we see the person and house drawings of Charles. He included a "lollypop" tree and flowers with his house. Charles is nine years old and has excellent motor coordination. His speech is good, but he is not very flexible or inventive. To the contrary, he is typically slow, fixed in his ideas, and highly dependent. Notice his emphasis upon the mouth (oral dependency) and the umbilical dot on the house. The house, as a mother symbol, fills his world, and he strongly stays by her side whenever possible. The figure concept is typical for a child of three and a half to four and a half years of age, and therefore his IQ would be in the 40-50 range at best. He is severely retarded in development.

In figure 52, a figure drawing typical of Russell, an institutionalized twenty-one-year-old male, is shown. His person drawing is at best that of a typical five-year-old. Note the extreme contrast between his figure and the "Bride" drawn by Ann who was five years at the time and had an IQ in the 130-140 range.

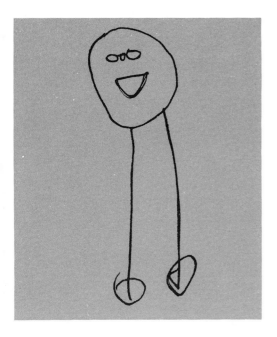

above: **Figure 50.** "Person" by Charles, 9 years

above right: **Figure 51.** "House" by Charles, 9 years.

right: **Figure 52.** "Person" by Russell, 21 years

far right: **Figure 53.** "Bride" by Ann, 5 years

Russell was not institutionalized until just before his legal birthday. In his home neighborhood he had made many friends and usually spent his days riding his bicycle about the streets or working part time in a sheltered workshop. He is a well-mannered person and reflects a fine home where the family members were aware of his needs and responded in a positive way to meet those needs. He may be expected to act in a responsible manner in any stable environment where some guidance is available.

The general maturation of the mentally deficient child is often clearly evidenced through the form development which we have found typical for normal children. In essence we may state that mentally deficient children progress through the same developmental pattern as young normal children. They progress, however, at a much slower rate and very rarely move beyond the schematic stage of seven to nine years. Figures 54 and 55 are drawings by John, a ten-year-old boy with Down's syndrome. It is evident that he has moved from the circular form into the vertical and horizontal character of the cross form. From his form in art we may suggest that he is resolving tasks and identifying generally with a normal development at three to four years of age.

Gaitskell (1953) noted in a survey of the drawing characteristics of mentally deficient children, who were all over six years of age, that the most severely retarded (IQ to 22) were generally completely passive when given crayons. A couple of these children scribbled after some encouragement, and a few others tried to eat the crayons. Those with higher intelligence (IQ 28-43) tended to draw with better control, and a noticeable development from disordered to circular scribbling appeared in their activity. He concluded from his study that

Figure 54. "Our House with Daddy's Room" by John, 10 years.

Figure 55. "Man" by John, 10 years

only those with an IQ over 40 would really benefit from art activity. Perhaps many teachers and therapists would be in disagreement with his view, as there are evident values in both the swinging arc scribble and the circular scribble.

A general lack of self-identification is typical in the simple figure concept of the mentally deficient child, and a poor social adaptation will follow as it is expressed first in a poor gestalt organization of the drawing surface, and then poor or late arrival, at best, of a schematic space. Figure 56 is a "family" drawn by Carol, a severely retarded child of nine years. Her figures tend to spatially "float" in a manner typical for a normal child of five to six years of age. It indicates that at nine years she has not as yet fully resolved the task of ego-closure and of becoming a social participant in her environment. It also indicates that she is not ready to read even though great stress is placed upon that task in her classroom.

Dorothy, a moderately retarded child of ten years, drew the landscape in figure 57. Her art behavior is characterized by strong repetition of subjects with only slight variation. The space of her picture indicates a schematic develop-

Figure 56. "Family" by Carol, 9 years

Figure 57. Landscape by Dorothy, 10 years.

ment, and she will be capable of "educable" tasks in the classroom. She will probably remain in a strong schematic character all of her life, and her art will continue to be typically haptic. At best it will become more decorative and rhythmical with proper motivation. It is seldom found that any mentally deficient individual will discover a capacity for expressing spatial depth or motion. Relative positioning or overlapping may be found with a few, but even they will never discover relative size and linear perspective. Our basic approach to encouraging these children in art must be through their haptic perceptual means and through the physical and emotional methods typically employed in work with younger children.

Recognizing the characteristics of mental deficiency in art behavior presents little difficulty. The child may express much of the following to a greater or lesser degree:

1. A retarded rate of growth but a normal pattern of growth.
2. Simple or primitive form but good motor coordination.
3. Lack of experimentation expressed in perseveration of form and subject.
4. Poor spatial gestalt characteristics indicating a lack of energy expended for association in the perceptual task.
5. Haptic-type experiencing as expressed in:
   a. A body-self centering of viewpoint regarding the space of the drawing or painting.
   b. Piece-method approach to modeling.
   c. Lack of spatial depth in drawing or painting.
   d. Bold, continuous-line character in drawing.
   e. Emotional exaggeration, omission, or distortion of form when motivated with a particular experience.
   f. Emotional use of color.
   g. Expression of tactual and kinesthetic awareness.

From these characteristics we may note the following basic needs:

1. A need to be sensitized to form and space.
2. A need for enrichment of concepts.
3. A need for more flexible use of concepts.
4. A need for deeper emotional sensitivity.
5. A need for social confidence.

Strategies for Enriched Experiencing Through Art

Attempting to deal directly with the mental functioning of the mentally deficient child would be similar to trying to teach a paraplegic to pole vault. We would be much wiser to work through the stronger physical and emotional channels, which, as we have already noted in the normal child, lead to concept formation. Our initial efforts must be directed toward a richer physical and emotional sensitivity. This course of action will be less frustrating for both the child and the teacher-therapist because it is the most natural course and draws upon the child's strengths rather than his weaknesses.

Large motor games should be stressed for all mentally deficient children, but especially in the early years. Lateness of motor development is one of the first indicators of mental deficiency, and we know already how crucial motor experimentation is to discovering form and space. The child actually learns to time objects and experience form in space by moving his own body through space. Experiencing his own body in space is also imperative to every child's most rudimentary self-identification, for the idea of self is only gained by interaction with other things and people in the environment. Because the mentally deficient child lacks an energy level for this exploratory experiencing, we must force it upon him in such a way that he must or will react.

The small infant may be rocked and thus experience passively a kinesthetic activity. Later we may swing him or roll with him in playing on the floor. He will have to be encouraged to shred paper, pull things out of boxes, and do many other things that normal children do without encouragement. (In fact, normal children are usually disciplined for such great things.) Care must be exercised in our efforts with the mentally deficient child, however, *that things move at a rate which allows him to follow or take part.* The more we can entice him to initiate in the activity, the greater its value will be to him.

Manipulative games which involve the visual senses are the best early games, for as we have seen, visual perception develops from motor activity. Holding a rubber ball in one's hands and then rolling it back and forth on the floor is a very meaningful experience. Eventually, watching it bounce will allow the child to "time and space" it with his own body.

Objects which are suspended from the ceiling will move and thus be watched, and it may be possible that the child could move or hit them himself.

Walking and running are normal rhythmic functions of the body, and games may be structured to encourage a more sensitive identification in such activities of bodily motion. Playground devices such as swings, seesaws, and climbing bars are excellent, but even walking on a stone wall or jumping across the cracks in the sidewalk may be a great game with mentally deficient children.

Playing the games will not only sensitize the child perceptually, but it will also begin to give him emotional confidence and build a healthy bridge between the child and the parent. Too many mentally deficient children cling to the parent physically and emotionally with no distance between for a bridge.

Along with the games, the child should be encouraged to scribble with a heavy black crayon on a typing-size paper. The drawing activity will provide one more kinesthetic reference and will also provide a very fine record of his progress.

The mentally deficient child may be expected to remain in the scribbling stage far beyond the norm for his chronological age. This should be looked upon as a greater opportunity to strengthen the physical confidence and the emotional security of the child.

The child also needs to own things and be responsible for them. Animals are one of the best experiences for a mentally deficient child. Owning and taking care of a dog or cat is a wonderful experience for any child, but it is particularly significant for this type of child. He will tend to identify in and through the pet, and his experiences with a pet will often act as a strong emotional reference for the space outside his own body.

When concepts are first recognized in the drawing of simple representational forms, we must begin to carefully sensitize the child to his body-self in order to enrich the developing schema with more details. A painful experience may especially be opportunity for verbally motivating a drawing. A cold, a toothache, a stubbed toe, a cut finger—any one of a number of these common experiences may provide a basis for sensitizing the child to a richer bodily concept. Notice in the work of Larry, a severely retarded nine-year-old boy, what simple verbal motivation can effect. In figure 58 we note his typical figure concept. It is a simple person with no torso and few details. In figure 59 we see the result of simple motivation concerning combing his hair in the morning and putting his new boots on. After a number of motivated drawing experiences we find his figure concept has become very rich in details (fig. 60). Even Billy's cat (fig. 61) is smiling.

above left: **Figure 58.** "Boy" by Larry, 9 years.

above: **Figure 59.** "Combing My Hair with My Big Boots On. There Are Muscles in My Arm" by Larry, 9 years.

left: **Figure 60.** "Me Smiling" by Larry, 9 years.

Figure 61. "Billy's Cat Is Smiling" by Larry, 9 years.

Another boy, Danny, who suffers from Down's syndrome, drew the rich figure of his father with a great many details. Such an accomplishment earlier would have been considered impossible (fig. 62).

Figure 62. "My Daddy" by Danny, 10 years

Puppets are a wonderful activity for the mentally deficient child. Construction of the puppet should be from simple materials such as a paper lunch bag or a paper plate with the face drawn on or made from pasted-on scraps of colored construction paper. The bag may be stuffed with paper and tied at the bottom on a stick, while the paper plate face may be glued or taped to a stick. Old stockings work well also as a basic puppet form. Older children may be capable of making a fist puppet from papier-mâché formed on a balloon. A body or clothing is not usually too important to the child, and we must remember that as a rule his attention span is short and he will be anxious to use his puppet just as soon as he can.

Puppet productions encourage the mentally deficient child to identify roles and respond to them. He may thoroughly enjoy standing in a corner, with one puppet on each hand, talking with the puppets. A "puppet corner" is a good idea for such activity in a classroom or therapy room. A simple stage may be made from a tipped-up table or from a large cardboard carton with a window cut in the front and a door in the back. From such a vantage point the child may thoroughly enjoy talking with his audience. A shy child may be found to often open up and begin to interact more freely from such experiences. Any similar group experience is to be encouraged, for the mentally deficient child will respond well socially as a rule when provided the opportunity from an early age. Because the physical and emotional potential is usually normal in the mentally deficient child, we find it most appropriate to encourage and strengthen him through those channels for greater social adeptness.

Opportunity for sensitivity to material characteristics may be provided for the child through various craft activities which will also serve as a means for developing finer manipulative skills. As with the normal child, the product becomes more important to the individual with advancing age, and he will seek recognition and approval for his efforts.

A salt-flour mix using one cup of salt, one cup of flour, and one tablespoon of powdered alum provides an excellent modeling mix suitable for mosaic activity (fig. 63). The ingredients should be mixed dry and then water slowly stirred in until the mix is smooth and about the consistency of cookie dough. For a small mosaic the mixture may be packed into the lid of a cottage cheese container to form a flat "cake." The design is then added by pushing in marbles, buttons, broken tiles, or other similar nonmetallic materials. Food coloring may be added to the mix, when stirring, for a strong contrast in the product later.

Sandcasting in cottage cheese cartons or old shoe boxes is another wonderful experience and provides a base for strong tactual sensitivity. For this experience, sand or fine sawdust is dampened and packed into the form up to about an

Figure 63.   Salt-flour mix mosaic

inch from the top of the container. Various objects like bark, acorns, stones, and shells are then pushed face down into the surface. Plaster is poured in to fill the form to the top, and then anxious moments pass to wait for the plaster to set that the cast might be removed. A wire (fig. 64) may be inserted before the plaster sets in order to provide a means for hanging the casting on a wall or fence later.

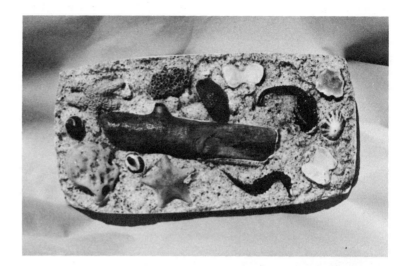

Collage activity is a similar experience for sensitizing the child, not only to tactual factors, but to the surface space as well. In figure 66 we see a collage started by gluing yarn to a piece of cardboard. Various types of beans, straws, and macaroni were then glued in with a casein glue which will be transparent when dry.

above: **Figure 64.** Cottage cheese box sandcasting.

above right: **Figure 65.** Shoe box sandcasting.

right: **Figure 66.** Yarn, macaroni, and bean collage.

Very simple weaving may be experienced by the mentally deficient child at an older age. The primary benefits of such activity are found in the fine manipulative skills necessary for the task and in the value of the product. In figure 67 we note a simple mat made by wrapping yarn around a piece of cardboard and then tying the intersecting points with string. After that step, the yarn is cut at the edges of the cardboard to produce a fringe. Pull and tie designs in colored burlap are a similar experience, and while the product is not usually as valuable in a utilitarian sense, it does provide an interesting aesthetic design when used as a wall-hanging.

Jewelry is a good activity with mentally deficient children of any age. The younger child is capable of rolling the salt-flour mix into beads and putting them on round toothpicks mounted on a styrofoam sheet to dry. They can then be pulled off within a day or two, painted and varnished, and strung to wear. Magazines may be cut by older children into long diamond shapes, folded in the center on a round toothpick, rolled up, and finally glued. When varnished and strung, they make a very attractive necklace (fig. 68).

left: **Figure 67.** Woven mat or pad

below: **Figure 68.** Magazine bead necklace.

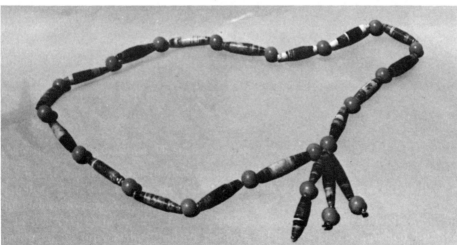

REFERENCES

BASKIN, JACQUELINE. "Retarded Children Need Art." *School Arts*, March 1955.

BELGAU, FRANK. *A Motor Perceptual Developmental Handbook of Activities*. La Porte, Texas: Perception Development Research Associates, 1966.

BENDER, LAURETTA. *Child Psychiatric Techniques*. Springfield, Ill.: Charles C Thomas, Publisher, 1952.

GAITSKELL, CHARLES and MARGARET. *Art Education for Slow Learners*. Peoria, Ill.: Chas. A. Bennett Co., Inc., 1953.

GOODENOUGH, FLORENCE. *The Measurement of Intelligence by Drawings*. New York: Harcourt, Brace and World, 1926.

GOSLIN, JANE. "Students Bring Art to Retarded Adults." *School Arts*, May 1959.

KIRK, S. A., and JOHNSON, G. F. *Educating the Retarded Child*. New York: Houghton Mifflin Co., 1951.

MATTIL, EDWARD. *Meaning in Crafts*. Englewood Cliffs, N. J.: Prentice-Hall, 1959.

PRESIDENT'S PANEL ON MENTAL RETARDATION. *Mental Retardation*. Washington, D. C.: U. S. Printing Office, 1963.

RANDALL, ARNE. "Art Time for Exceptional Children." *School Arts*, April 1952.

SARASON, SEYMOUR. *Psychological Problems in Mental Deficiency*. New York: Harper and Brothers, 1949.

STRINGHAM, LUTHER, et al. *Mental Retardation*. Washington, D. C.: Committee on Mental Retardation, USOE. Printed by U. S. Government Printing Office, 1963.

WANKELMAN, WILLARD F.; WIGG, MARIETTA; and WIGG, PHILIP R. *Handbook of Arts and Crafts for Elementary and Junior High School Teachers*. 2nd ed. Dubuque, Ia.: Wm. C. Brown Company Publishers, 1968.

4 The Physically Impaired Child and Art

Earlier the significance of somatic experiencing was emphasized as a sole premise for reality structuring. All experiences from which reality is formed are communicated through the body. We have just noted the tremendous difficulties of the child with a weakened brain capability which has its effect in a slower flow of communicated experiencing. We will now recognize that most other somatic impairments will not decrease the flow of such communication, *but they will present a distortion of such experience to the mind.* The physically impaired child will "see" in an atypical manner, and we may generally recognize him as perceptually handicapped in either the receptive physical sense or in the apperceptive residual sense. Our discussion will consider the implications of an orthopedic handicap for the experiencing of the child in art and then move on to view similar factors in children with neurological handicap, visual handicap, and auditory handicap.

The Child with an Orthopedic Handicap

Most orthopedic impairments are easily recognized by observation, and our initial problem is therefore not one of recognizing that an individual suffers from such a difficulty of function. Such disability, however, may more severely handicap the child if he is unable to emotionally and consciously accept his impaired status. Indeed, an orthopedic inability of function actually becomes a *handicap* when the unconscious mind resists recognition of the loss of bodily function. This may occur when the individual is emotionally overwhelmed by the loss of function or to some degree when a social awareness is deeply felt. When conscious acceptance of the physical status is forthcoming, an adequate means of compensation is usually reached, and the individual rapidly learns to recognize and cope with the typical tasks of life which confront most of us who deal with an orthopedic impairment.

Minor physical impairments, perhaps even imaginary ones, may seriously handicap children and be expressed as major problems in the projected body-image. Adolescents, for example, who we know are those with the lowest mortality rate by far, are proven to be those with the highest absenteeism. They are at once the healthiest and the "sickest." They are confronted with a changing body which is difficult to accept emotionally. Our emphasis of orthopedic impairment will be upon the projected image of the self in drawing, for in that image we will note the emotional secondary effects which most usually, and more severely, handicap the child.

If somatic function is impaired, the body-image will itself be distorted as the child views his immediate bodily environment with an emotional bias for the disabled part. The type and degree of distortion will depend upon the actual impairment and the child's response, in terms of acceptance or rejection, to the impairment. In a severe injury the child may or may not accept, within himself, even his self-existence. A girl who was suffering from complete paralysis due to a neck fracture awoke in the hospital to ask the doctor, "Do you have any reality pills?" A few weeks later during a film, she suddenly shouted out in a darkened room, "I'm alive, I'm alive!" She had finally been able to accept, to a small degree at least, her real status.

Lowenfeld (1947) was one of the first writers to notice expression of physical impairment in drawings of the human figure. He found that continuous exaggeration, omissions, or distortions of the same body part usually pointed to a defect or abnormality of that particular body part. It is important to note that such projection in the body-image *must be consistent*. We have already noted in the motivated drawings of children without physical impairment how they exaggerate and distort form to express emotional significance in a particular experience. The physically impaired child will consistently project irregularities in self-image without such motivation.

Research of the projected body-image of physically impaired children has placed emphasis upon the importance of having the child draw himself rather than just a "man." Martorana (1954) found in her study of orthopedically involved children that ninety-four percent of her population drew normal figures in response to the Goodenough "draw-a-man" technique. When the same population was asked to draw a self-portrait, seventy-two percent of the children revealed their impairment by exaggerations, omissions, or distortions of form in the projected body-image. Centers and Centers (1963) found similar results in their study of amputee children.

In figure 69 we note a kindergarten child's self-portrait with an exaggerated left arm in the projected body-image. He was very aware, and proud, of the cast on his broken arm.

Figure 69.   Self-portrait by Raymond, 5 years

The girl who drew the self-portrait in figure 70 was not proud, and certainly not as consciously aware, of her physical impairment. She is six years old and suffers a total paralysis to one side of her body. In her drawing we note first that she placed the projected left hand directly on the shoulder instead of on an arm as is the case with the right hand. If we look more closely at the projected left hand, we will notice that she originally erased a line behind the lowest finger. That line had extended horizontally beyond the present finger and then it dropped vertically down. If we for a moment consider the projected left side

Figure 70. Self-portrait by Donna, 6 years [lines darkened]

according to the original linear structure, we will recognize that it was similar to the present projected right side. She had originally drawn a figure with two right sides since she was unaware of, or perhaps "blocked out," the left side. Her situation in regard to acceptance of the "dead" part of her body is very similar to that of a person with cerebral damage, for instance in a stroke, which destroys awareness of half of the body-self.

An example of all three means for expressing unconscious awareness of physical impairment is evidenced in the self-portraits by Charles (figs. 71, 72, and 73). The first drawing (fig. 71) was produced in September on the first day of school, and his corrected clubfoot is indicated by a "squared off" toe on the shoe. While such distortion is slight, it is significant. The second drawing (fig. 72) was made in January, and here he exaggerates the foot in size. The final drawing (fig. 73) was produced in May of the same school year, and in this drawing he omits the feet. Notice, also, his tendency to draw the projected left leg narrower than the right leg. It is evident that Charles is affected by a very minor impairment which has little effect physically but a major effect psychically. He needs to be carefully drawn out in expressing his deeper unconscious feelings about himself through art. By a simple extension of his reference of experience concerning himself, a catharsis or therapy may be performed in the emotional sphere of his life.

Figure 71. Self-portrait by Charles, 11 years.

Figure 72. Self-portrait by Charles, 11 years.

Figure 73. Self-portrait by Charles, 11 years.

In figure 74 we see a contrast to Charles in the work of Linda, a girl with severe athetoid-type cerebral palsy, who, while severely impaired physically, is not handicapped emotionally by her condition. She is of normal intelligence and produces above-average work in school. She has been aided in establishing meaningful experiences, and her acceptance of her physical status is excellent. She simply needs encouragement in performing within her physical limitations.

Figure 74. Self-portrait by Linda, 11 years.

Particular material experiences in art would be impossible to state for the general group of children who are orthopedically impaired. Specific manipulative needs are found with many, while others are physically capable in any art material. Painting and drawing are generally excellent whether the child draws normally with his hand or has the tool strapped to his foot. Felt-tipped pens are probably the best overall drawing tool, as they leave a strong line with little pressure and never need to be refilled. Soft lead pencils and ball-point pens have this same advantage and provide the opportunity for more detail.

The Neurologically Handicapped Child

When some organic occurrence causes a permanent-type dysfunction of a child's brain, his mind will experience distorted communications of material reality. If he is of normal intelligence, such communication will be transmitted at a normal rate, and the degree and type of distortion will be determined basically by the location and severity of the brain damage. In cases of very minor dysfunction the child may produce unacceptable social behaviors and suffer extreme learning difficulties. We will point out very carefully how such a child may be recognized, and aided, through art. With cases of major dysfunction it is imperative that we discuss the experiencing of the child, for we often become frustrated with his inability to learn or to perform even a simple task. He may, at the same time, be confused and frustrated primarily with a lack of bodily awareness and control.

A history of "label-making" for the neurologically handicapped child readily reveals understandings of his true experiencing. The knowledge which has been obtained is very recent when we compare this type of exceptional child to most other groups. Too many children with neurological handicap continue even today to ambulate along in a normal classroom where they are "passed over" or "put up with." The more severely involved child may be placed in a special classroom for the "educationally handicapped" where he may be commonly considered "retarded" or "schizophrenic."

In the past the term *brain injury* has been popularly used for any individual with neurological handicap. Such an "exogenous" label set the neurologically handicapped apart from those who suffered functional disturbances of personality and also from those who could be considered familial or endogenous mental deficients. The term *brain injury* implies a normal or superior brain capability which has been impaired through accident or disease. A child may have suffered undue hemorrhaging of the brain in the birth process. He may have sustained injury through a childhood fall, a high fever during illness with measles, or even a lack of oxygen at some time. The actual origin of injury is seldom determined. Toxic poisoning is a slow but deadly cause of brain impairment, also, and our society is just now discovering what we have been doing to the common environment from which all of us feed. In addition, children too often can easily get into the common household stores of pesticides and fertilizers.

A few of the earlier researchers, such as Head (1926) and Hebb (1942), emphasized the general or gestalt function of the brain. Their studies indicate that in some cases a person might lose, through surgical removal, a damaged portion of the brain and function in a perfectly normal manner. The healthy brain apparently would take over the function of the absent portion. If the unhealthy portion were left, however, it would in many cases cause a dysfunction of the larger brain mass. This is essentially what occurs in the condition we call neurological handicap.

With time the term *brain-injured* was noted to apply not only to cases of known organic dysfunction but to a broader syndrome of behavioral manifestations as well. Strauss (1947) used the term to speak of children with disturbances of perception, thinking, and social behavior. Many, today, still use the label "Strauss syndrome" for the neurologically handicapped child. Strauss and Werner (1942) were particularly interested in the disturbed perception of the child with neurological handicap. Such distortion makes it almost impossible for some children to produce forms in drawing. Being able to move a point to produce a line which will then meet the original starting point is a simple task for most of us. However, such a task calls for keen motion perception. From the gestalt researches of the past, we know that the time-space factors of motion perception depend basically upon bodily awareness and the interaction of the body-self with objects in the environment. The child with neurological handicap is not "tuned" spatially and temporally with his environment, and he is often not even strongly aware of his own bodily weight, position, and mass. When we once begin to realize this fact, then we are starting to identify with the manner in which he experiences and the extreme handicap which his physical status forces upon him.

The body space-time kinesthesis of the child was studied by Bender (1943), and she developed her Visual-Motor Gestalt Test as a primary means for assessing perceptual-motor function. Closure abilities in producing forms and proximities of form are basic considerations in the test. Children with neurological handicap will often be found to "fragment" and rotate forms in copying the visual gestalten figures. The recent work by Koppitz (1964) is especially noteworthy as a reference for using the Bender Test with young children.

Hanvik (1961) has used the term *cerebral dysfunction* for the child with neurological handicap, and from this popular term we often hear of a child with normal or superior intelligence referred to as having "minimal cerebral dysfunction." Or he may be called a "mentally defective normal." Such a term is excellent because it not only properly recognizes the impairment but also emphasizes the child's true potential.

The overt behavioral manifestations of the neurologically handicapped child are often misinterpreted socially, and it is from that reference that he has been labeled "the other child." His behavior may be characterized by hyperactivity, temper tantrums, involuntary or irregular motor actions, and a fascination for certain objects. He may be very distracted or drawn to a bright shiny object or a noise—especially a rhythmic sound with which he can associate physically. He will enjoy "tuning in." He may express himself in irregular speech or with seemingly detached thoughts. Many neurologically handicapped children tend to withdraw from social contact, or simply cannot identify with it, and thus may appear withdrawn or even autistic.

Goldstein (1942) noted the tendency for perseveration in the child with neurological handicap, and we may best identify with this behavioral expression in the child's desire to seek the familiar. New things are often frightening, as well as frustrating. It is not unusual for the child to turn from a new experience or attack an object with a burst of energy; most organisms will respond in the same way. The child with neurological handicap needs great security and assurance. Reading is most frustrating for him due to his disturbed perception, and it is not unusual to find him reversing or rotating letters.

Proper assessment of neurological handicap must be made. The evaluation must be thorough in order to discover abilities as well as limitations. Only a complete neuropsychiatric work-up may be called adequate. Often such an examination appears costly to the parents but is really an inexpensive step in the long run. If we value the human life, and esteem the contribution that a life may hold for society, it is a small price to pay. Proper medication and treatment will usually provide dramatic changes, especially in the younger child with a minimal dysfunction. Without proper assessment and treatment the child remains in a status where he is very prone to emotional detachment due to his poor grasp of reality. As we will see in our final chapter, what at first often appears to be a purely functional disturbance may have a deeper and more basic organic etiology. Too many children with neurological handicap, of years gone by, are now terminating their lives in our mental and penal institutions—to our shame.

Understanding Dysfunction Through Drawing

Since the awareness of the body-self is most basically affected in neurological handicap, it is to be expected that the projected body-image in art will again hold clues for an exceptional condition.

Pfister (1934) noted that heavier line pressure was applied in the drawings produced by organically involved patients. This was later supported by Buck (1948) and Jolles (1964). Bender (1940) found that a Goodenough score two years or more below the Binet score would make the individual child suspect for neurological handicap (see figs. 75 and 76). Bender also noted that the inability to draw the human figure may not extend to other subjects. Buck (1948), Jolles (1964), Machover (1949), Vernier (1952), and Hammer (1955) all suggested criteria in the H-T-P drawing technique for neurological handicap. Much speculation, debate, and retesting of the criteria followed, and much conjecture remains today from some of these proposed diagnostic criteria. Most subsequent study lends credibility or clarification to the use of the H-T-P as an appropriate and valuable tool for assessment of neurological handicap. Especially significant is its use for screening purposes and then as a diagnostic part in test batteries.

Figure 75. Person by Jim, 6 years. Verbal IQ 126 and Performance IQ 106.

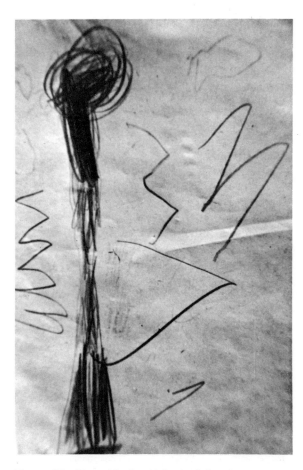

Figure 76. "Tree Hit by Lightning" by Jim, 6 years

Michal-Smith (1953) compared H-T-P drawings of adult patients with normal electroencephalographic tracings to those with abnormal tracings and found that "line quality" was a valid criterion. It is later mentioned in study by Cohn (1960) as "linear perseveration" or redrawing. Reznikoff and Tomblen (1956) found five criteria to differentiate between emotionally disturbed patients and patients who were organically impaired: weak synthesis, parts misplaced, shrunken arms and legs, parts other than the head and extremities distorted, and petal-like or scribbled fingers.

In 1960 Cohn made perhaps the most extensive study of drawing characteristics for judging neurological handicap. His population numbered 8,000 subjects, and his results substantiated many of the earlier proposed criteria. His criteria were as follows:

1. Distortion
2. Asymmetry
3. Perseveration
4. Simplification.

He notes that distortion involves a disproportionate configuration or "disarrangement" of body parts. His term *perseveration* regarded redrawing so as to "represent by intertwining and overlapped repetitions of line where a single line would usually suffice." This, of course, would suggest the use of erasing as well. His term *simplification* concerned a more primitive figure and not just a stick man. It was wise of Cohn to tell his subjects to draw "the picture of a person, front view, the entire person." Imbalances are thus easily seen.

In drawing upon the previously stated writings and from other conducted research, this writer (1969) has concluded that the following criteria are of benefit in discerning neurological handicap in children through their drawings:

1. Asymmetry in the projected body-image
2. Distortion and rotation of form
3. Redrawing and erasing (perseveration)
4. Weak synthesis of parts
5. Heavy line pressure
6. Primitive wholes.

The final criterion would apply basically to the more severely involved children. Personal familiarity with the drawings of known cases of neurological handicap is perhaps most beneficial, as even here, in our attempt to be objective, we must realize the strong subjectivity which naturally comes into play with each observer.

In figure 77 we note a person drawn by Robin, a six-year-old girl with very poor motor coordination. The erratic line production and poor closure of shapes are typical for the neurologically handicapped child.

Figure 77. Person by Robin, 6 years.

Diabetes insipidus was responsible for the high fever which caused brain-damage to Jack (fig. 78). At sixteen years he was attempting to draw a football player. Notice again the poor motor coordination and the poor line closure.

At seven years Steven drew his "best boy" in figure 79. He was an aphasic child with no speech but good motor coordination. A high fever during a case of the measles caused his condition. At ten years of age he again drew a "best boy" (fig. 80) and little change can be noted. He expresses himself in primitive mandala-like figures which rotate to a considerable degree.

Figure 78. Football player by Jack, 16 years

Figure 79. "Best Boy" by Steven, 7 years

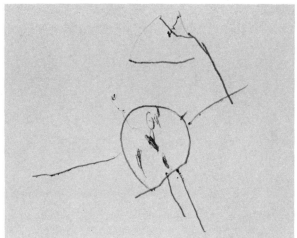

Figure 80. "Best Boy" by Steven, 10 years.

The six-year-old girl who drew figure 81 expresses extreme confusion of the body-self. She is severely impaired in the perceptual process, and most of our drawing criteria may be evidenced in her human figure drawing. Many today prefer to call the neurologically handicapped child by the term *perceptually handicapped*. The term is very appropriate, for as Laura Lehtinen states, "This damage has changed the way in which he perceives the world."

In Donald's human figure drawing (fig. 82) we note the tremendous drawing and redrawing which often occur in the projection of the body-image. He is an extremely hyperactive boy in spite of heavy medication. His reading is poor. Like most children with neurological handicap, he has his "good days" and his "bad days." He verbalizes well but is extremely poor in motor tasks.

Figure 81. Person by girl 6 years

Figure 82. Person by Donald, 9 years

Ralph's figure drawing (fig. 83) reveals a very weak synthesis of the body parts and asymmetry in the projected body-image.

The figure drawn by Ray (fig. 84) was actually his fourth try. The third try is erased on the same plate. In figure 85 we note his first try and second try. He was twelve years old at the time and had been referred for psychological testing due to his undisciplined manner in a normal classroom.

Figure 83. Person by Ralph, 10 years

Figure 84. Person by Ray, 12 years

Figure 85. Person by Ray, 12 years

The person presented in figure 86 is by Ted, a sixteen-year-old boy. Here we notice strong asymmetry in the body-image. It seems that he does not know how long his right arm and leg should be. The brain injury in his case was localized in the left hemisphere which controls the right side of the body.

Peter, a bright ten-year-old boy with very minor dysfunction, drew the person and tree in figures 87 and 88. Notice the static projection of the left arm. His injury was localized in the right cerebral hemisphere.

above: **Figure 86.**   Person by Ted, 16 years

above right: **Figure 87.**   Person by Peter, 10 years

right: **Figure 88.**   Tree by Peter, 10 years

Effects of Medical Therapy on NH Art

Since neurological handicap is a basic physical impairment, it is logical to first consider for the child therapy benefits from the field of medicine. In a few cases we might find a physician recommending surgery, but for the most part various medications are prescribed. Two typical cases of neurological handicap will be reviewed as a means for describing the child, recognition of his impairment, and the effects of medication in producing H-T-P drawings.

STEVEN

At seven years of age Steven was a puzzling child to both his parents and his teacher. He was a well-mannered boy who came from a fine home. His parents were college graduates, and he undoubtedly had a fine intelligence. Yet he was having extreme difficulty in reading, and his motor coordination was poor enough that he was noticed to be "clumsy." It was noted that he often could not recall simple words that were spoken just the day before, and his thought pattern seemed to be quite unusual. He was referred to the school psychologist who stated, "Steven's problem is an atypical one and so far remains undiagnosed. It may be a late maturing characteristic, or something more obscure. . . ." He was noted to have gross perceptual difficulties when copying the Bender figures.

The first H-T-P figures Steven drew are seen in figures 89 and 90. The projected right arm is elongated, and the same factor is even more exaggerated in the tree limb which moves out the upper left corner of the drawing surface. The figure is basically a "primitive whole" and, in this regard, below what we would expect for his age and intelligence. The house form in figure 90 indicates motion perception difficulty through poor line closure. Even the placement of the house on the paper is unusual. The facial features on the human figure were difficult for Steven to produce. In the drawing task he used his left hand, but it was evident that he preferred his right hand for other activities.

An electroencephalograph test was arranged for Steven, and the tracings indicated the following:

Diffuse irregular continuous mixed alpha-theta wave activity of moderate high to moderate and low voltages with a generous amount of bursty high voltage delta waves occurring in all leads . . . temporal asynchrony . . . hyperventila-

Figure 89. Combined H-T-P by Steven, 7 years

Figure 90. Person and House by Steven, 7 years

tion—increased the delta activity with some showing associated abortive spike potentials.

The diagnosis was as follows:

> Diffuse dysrrhythmic EEG mildly abnormal for a seven year, 9 month old subject. Tracings are not specific but convulsive susceptibility is suggested.

Steven was placed on a three-quarter grain of dilantin for six weeks as a beginning to drug therapy. At the end of that period of time Steven drew another H-T-P series.

While the second series of drawings were produced in crayon, a noticeable change in the projected body-image has occurred (figs. 91, 92, and 93). The improvement in a stable feeling of symmetry is obvious. The right foot of the human figure is larger than the left foot, but otherwise the placement and integration of body parts is excellent. If medication is continued, Steven probably will be much improved in his total referencing and achievement in a few months' time.

right: **Figure 91.**   House by Steven, 7 years

below: **Figure 92.**   Tree by Steven, 7 years

below right: **Figure 93.**   Person by Steven, 7 years

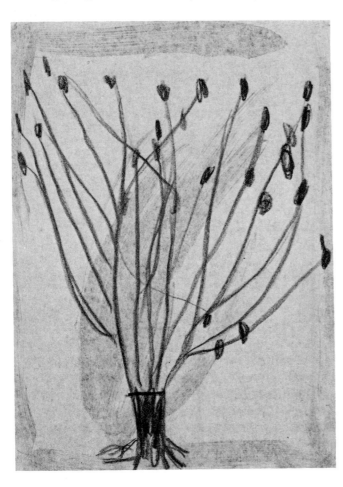

BRUCE

The etiology of Bruce's problem is a difficult one to trace. As an infant he was extremely passive. At six months he would do little more than turn his head. Testing at nine months indicated a normal intelligence but subnormal large motor activity. No physical problem was evident. He gradually became more active until at the age of three years he was described as a "human dynamo." His activity often resulted in injury which could possibly cause permanent damage to the cerebral cortex. When he was three, his sister chased him against a car and fell on him. He was unconscious for some time after the accident. Later on in school he was soon labeled for his hyperactivity. His noise and abuse of other children made it necessary to isolate him often from the rest of the class. Teachers' comments in his cumulative folder from the third grade through the sixth grade indicate the continuous overt behavior of Bruce: "Will push and pick on other children on the playground, seeks attention by misbehavior. Fails to cooperate in games. Shows temper if he doesn't get his way." "Still possesses his aggressive traits. Not inclined to be accepted by classmates." "Explodes now and then." "Has a long way to go yet."

His extreme behavior was the basis for further testing in the sixth grade. The report of the testing disclosed an IQ of 112, but the scores were found to be very uneven at the various mental levels—he missed many easy items at lower levels and more difficult items at the higher levels. Oral expression was very superior, but nonverbal areas and basic problem-solving tasks were concluded rather poorly. He was noted as being highly nervous with a low frustration tolerance. The WISC Performance Tests showed slight difficulty with visual-motor coordination, and during the Bender Test he rotated the paper even though his directional tendencies appeared adequate. He gave the examiner the feeling that "he would really like to be able to control himself better."

Bruce's H-T-P drawings (figs. 94, 95, and 96) were picked from a group as a suspect of neurological handicap. The teachers' comments and the cumulative folder data supported the observation. He was eleven years old at the time. A conference was arranged with the mother, who had been at wits end for years with "his incessant thumping." She said he would often reverse words in his speech with such comments as, "No one can else do it." His mother was given

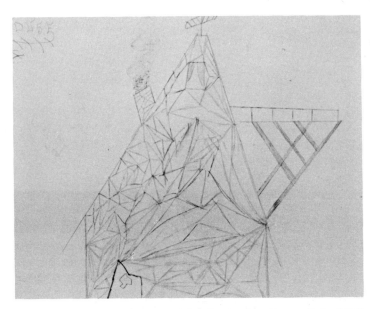

Figure 94. House by Bruce (1st H-T-P)

Figure 95. Tree by Bruce (1st H-T-P)

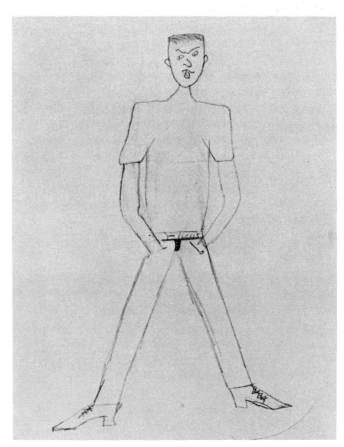

Figure 96. Person by Bruce (1st H-T-P)

a letter of referral for her family physician, and neurological tests were scheduled in San Francisco.

Bruce's H-T-P had revealed several significant signs of very minor neurological handicap. His attempt at drawing a house with a geodesic dome (fig. 94) was unusual, but only the emphasis on the porch was considered a possible imbalance. The tree drawing (fig. 95) suggests strong, impulsive character in the quickness of linear stroke, but the lack of match in the two sides indicates imbalance in the body-image. We might simply say that the left side is shorter. The difference in feeling for the two sides of the body is even more apparent in the human figure drawing (fig. 96). Here the left leg is noticeably shorter, and he drew a line beneath it in emphasizing that fact. The head is moved over on the axis of the body. A great deal of redrawing and erasing is evident in the original drawing. The shoelaces are prominently drawn and are an emotional symbol of castration. This could be considered somewhat typical for a prepubescent boy.

In the early neurological testing Bruce was given an arm deviation test which is a manual test of placing both arms in an extended forward position with the eyes closed. The task is to keep both arms and hands in a parallel horizontal position. Bruce would not even attempt the test without placing both thumbs together for a guide. The following EEG Test indicated "Spiking in the right temporal and associated bioccipital area more on the right." Bruce was started on dilantin which is one of the older and more predictable psychotherapeutic drugs. One month later he produced a second H-T-P series (figs. 97, 98, and 99).

The house (fig. 97) is quite well organized with no unusual characteristics of asymmetry. The two ends of the house do indicate the strength of the mother in the home. His tree (fig. 98) still has a shorter left side in the body-image projection. A swing, however, appears to balance this shortness or compensate for it. The human figure (fig. 99) is most interesting, as here we see a decided change in attitude. He has strengthened the edge of the face or self-image and the expression is that of a perplexed feeling. At this point Bruce had ceased to drum on things continually, and his efforts at throwing a tantrum often "fizzled out." The left leg in the projection is still shorter.

Figure 97. House by Bruce (1st H-T-P).

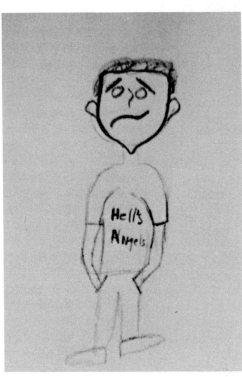

right: **Figure 98.** Tree by Bruce (2nd H-T-P).

far right: **Figure 99.** Person by Bruce (2nd H-T-P).

By the end of the seventh-grade year his cumulative folder for the first time contained some positive remarks: "Has improved greatly this year. Peers have remarked at his improvement." He began to do a bit of cartooning, and when a third H-T-P series was obtained a year later, the figures were almost rigid in their stylized character (figs. 100 and 101). They do appear well formed and balanced.

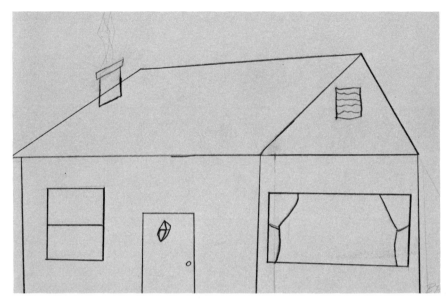

Figure 100. House by Bruce (3rd H-T-P)

Figure 101. Tree and Person by Bruce (3rd H-T-P).

Two years after medication was initiated, a final H-T-P series was obtained from Bruce who was now very irritated at the request. It was learned that he had not taken his medication for some time, and the drawings support this fact (figs. 102, 103, 104). The porch of the house is back along with the two ends. There are curtains in the windows suggesting a strong effeminate identity—his paranoid reaction is also good evidence of such an identity. The tree without foliage now suggests the barren state of his life, and the broken branch suggests a defeat. The squirrel indicates his dependency upon the mother. The human figure drawing (fig. 104) once again includes the shoelace emphasis. The body is overclothed, and the hands have short, impulsive fingers.

He was encouraged to continue his prescribed medication but became more belligerent with time. He stole autos and was sent to a facility of the California Youth Authority. He attempted suicide several times in subsequent years. Finally, at the age of eighteen, he attempted murder by stabbing another boy during an argument. He was again placed in a penal institution where he now resides. His case points up the importance of early and continued therapy. Early frustrations due to a slight neurological impairment slowly developed attitudes and values which carried Bruce outside the bounds of normal society.

We have noted that medication does offer a means for therapy and it does certainly affect, to some degree, the basic body-image character as we have seen it reflected in projective drawing. There are, however, many other avenues of aid, especially in art, where specific materials and activities may help correct the basic perceptual distortion which the neurologically handicapped child suffers.

right: **Figure 102.** House by Bruce (4th H-T-P).

below: **Figure 103.** Tree by Bruce (4th H-T-P).

below right: **Figure 104.** Person by Bruce (4th H-T-P).

Therapy Through Art Material Strategies

We know that the perceptual difficulties of the neurologically handicapped child make art activities of a two-dimensional type almost impossible. The fragmented type of rambling which we see in figure 105 is typical of the drawings of severely impaired children with neurological handicap. It is imperative that

Figure 105. Drawing by Betty, 16 years

we understand exactly what is disturbing the perceptual process, and then structure material activities which will, at least in part, correct the child's perceptual experiencing.

We know that motor incoordination and poor motion perception are often characteristic of the impairment. The matter of poor motion perception originates from a poor identification of physical awareness in one's own body, and improvement will come by a greater sensitivity to one's own bodily mass, weight, and positioning. Some of the same motor games which we previously mentioned with the mentally deficient child will be an aid in establishing such a sensitivity. Beyond these factors we must recognize other difficulties in perceptual experiencing.

We might note that the child, to begin with, tends to have greater sensitivity toward a surface *per se* since he cannot follow the motion of an object, or line, in relationship to its background. Ruben (1915) was the first to speak of the optic field in regard to object-ground relationship. Strauss and Werner (1942) devised tachistoscopic, visuo-motor, and tactual-motor tests to study normal and abnormal object-ground reactions. They found the child with neurological handicap uses a general "incoherent" approach perceptually, while the endogenous child uses a "global" approach. In a gestalt sense they were simply stating that the child with neurological handicap suffers from an inability to organize the perceptual field into a good gestalt configuration. We are simply stating that this results in a fragmented or disorganized aesthetic pattern in the drawing surface when he tries to express himself in art. Werner and Thuma (1942) in their study of the space-time abilities of the child through flicker-frequency experiences also noted that his abilities to perceive motion are highly impaired. It would seem from these studies that *art materials used with the child who has neurological handicap must be basically surface-oriented.* One study by Werner and Strauss (1942) noted this factor. They experimented with the gait of the child and found that the perceptually impaired child who could hardly walk in daylight could take almost normal steps by looking at his white shoes as he walked in the darkened room. He apparently could perceive the motion of a white or "negative" figure by its character as a "hole" in a dark or "positive" background.

This background of study has led us to investigate the effect that white drawing and painting materials may have on the neurologically handicapped child when they are used in combination with a dark surface. In figure 106 we note the person drawing by Ray, an eight-year-old boy with neurological handicap. The eyes slant to the right and the hair to the left. The figure is so imbalanced that it looks as though it may be dancing. In figure 107 we note his person drawing which was produced by using white crayon on a black paper. The human figure concept is more stable and richer in details. After several months of using white material on black surfaces, Ray was painting some fine pictures and thoroughly enjoying the experience (fig. 108). They were very rich in aesthetic quality.

right: **Figure 106.** Person by Ray, 8 years.

far right: **Figure 107.** Person by Ray, 8 years.

Figure 108. "Snowman" by Ray, 8 years.

As a result of this success, a study was formed to test the effect of such material combinations on a group of severely impaired children. Seventeen spastic cerebral-palsied children from four to nine years of age were selected as typically impaired in their perceptual abilities. They drew H-T-P figures with black crayon on twelve-by-eighteen-inch white paper and then with white crayon on black paper. The results were judged and statistically analyzed with a significant improvement noted in the second set of drawings at the one percent level of significance. In figures 109 and 110 we note one child's improvement in the figure drawing.

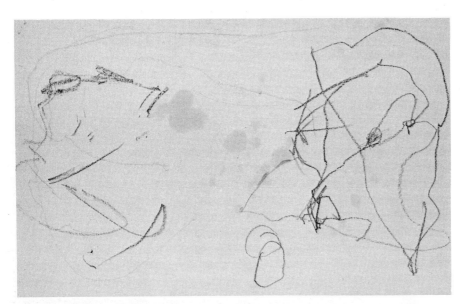

Figure 109.   Person by Marc, 7 years

Figure 110.   Person by Marc, 7 years

A child with a Sturge-Weber syndrome problem was tried subsequently with the same materials and the same results (figs. 111, 112, and 113). In figure 111 we note his attempt to draw a tree (lower left), a house (lower center), and a person (lower right). In figure 112 we note the improvement in the human figure by using white crayon on black paper and in figure 113 the improved house. It is evident from these examples that the child's perceptual experiencing may be dramatically improved by reversing the object-ground materials that are

Figure 111. H-T-P figures by Charles, 7 years.

Figure 112. Person by Charles, 7 years

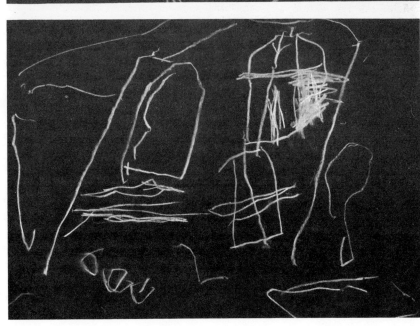

Figure 113. House by Charles, 7 years

typically used. It provides an opportunity for the child to produce a better gestalt image and a more aesthetic product.

Art activity for the neurologically handicapped child should involve materials of large size with tactual character and the use of a white figure or object on a dark ground or surface.

A salt-flour mix could be transformed into a dark material for mosaics by stirring in dark food coloring. After being packed into a cottage cheese lid, light-colored objects such as buttons, shells, or stones could be applied by the child to produce a picture.

Collage activity could be used successfully with the NH child by providing white objects to be glued onto a dark cardboard surface. Even white yarn or string could be "drawn" with on such a surface.

White metallic magnets could be used for a design means on a dark piece of metal. White yarn could be pinned to a dark sheet of Celotex for expressive purposes. Stitching with white yarn on dark burlap would be an excellent activity for a child with neurological handicap.

Crayon etching, in which light areas are scratched from a dark surface, would meet the needs of the perceptually impaired child. The crayon should be heavily applied over a white tagboard surface and then powdered with cornstarch and painted with india ink before scratching through.

The Child with a Visual Impairment

Loss of vision may or may not highly handicap the individual. The degree of handicapping will be determined basically by the type of perceptual experiencing and, to some extent, by age.

Lowenfeld (1947) has best clarified the two types of perceptual experiencing, appropriate to a discussion of the blind, through his terms *visual* and *haptic*. We are indebted to him as well for the basic understandings which will form our discussion of the blind child's art.

A visual person, we previously noted, was seen to be extroverted toward his environment and therefore *can be emphasized as a person who places great energy into the matter of organizing, in his mind, a total image of himself in respect to his immediate surroundings*. We can say, in short, that his self-image and feeling of identity are more dependent upon such interaction and organization. Essentially, the visual person will depend upon his eyes basically as a means for perception. If vision is destroyed, however, he will still tend to perceive *in the same manner* but will rely upon the other senses for perceptual communication. We must keep in mind, as Lowenfeld has noted, that "the blind individual can perceive objects that are larger than his hand only by moving his hand over the object." Loss of vision, it would appear, would therefore greatly impair the visual person. It does slow him down, and yet we must again recognize that he is putting tremendous energy into the task of integrating and organizing his perceptual space or field. As a result, the more visually-minded blind individual will usually have a better idea of total space when we compare him to his haptically-minded blind brother. The visual blind merely utilize nonvisual sensory communication for a visual-type perceptual experiencing, and as a result, they often adjust very well to their impairment.

The haptic blind do not place energy, to a high degree, into the task of discerning their own body in space. As a result, they poorly function in unifying their separate sensory communications to form a total idea or concept. Their view of space-time factors, necessary for motion perception, is often highly impaired. An experiment by Flores (1968) has pointed out the significance of this fact. The more haptic blind child in his study was found to be much slower in arriving at a total concept of the human figure and had great difficulty in integrating the parts of the figure in drawing. Some had to practice even a simple circular scribble at length before achieving the ability to draw a circle.

In Flores's study (1968) the visually-minded blind child often was highly successful in drawing a human figure after mild motivation. In figures 114, 115, 116, and 117 we note the successive improvement of such a child in drawing a

right: **Figure 114.** Visually-minded boy's drawing of a person—1st attempt (from Flores).

far right: **Figure 115.** Visually-minded boy's drawing of a person—2nd attempt (from Flores).

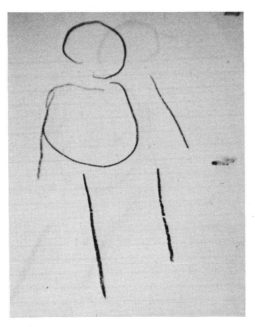
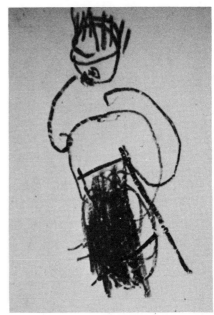

right: **Figure 116.** Visually-minded boy's drawing of a person—3rd attempt (from Flores).

far right: **Figure 117.** Visually-minded boy's drawing of a person—4th attempt (from Flores).

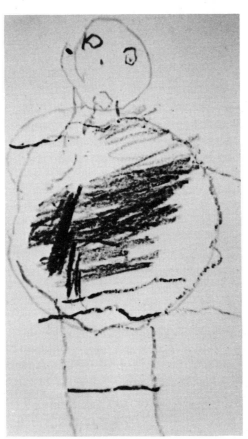
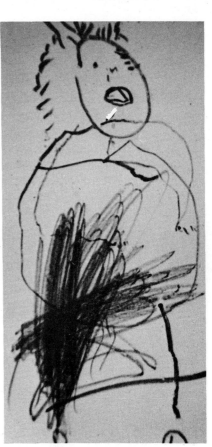

person. The evidence recalls Lowenfeld's words: "What the blind individual cannot always, or can only seldom achieve in life, he can do in art: out of the many partial impressions he builds up a 'whole' and arrives thus at a synthesis of his image." It is important for blind children to draw as well as model. In fact, Lowenfeld found that the younger children did not even know they were impaired and simply developed as any normal child would develop in the early physical-emotional experiencing of life. It is with age, after we have conditioned the perceptual needs of the child, that he may first realize the atypical character of his impairment and thus become handicapped.

Our treatment of the blind child is critically important in the early years. He must be led into experiencing which will help him to be independent and secure. *Such experiencing will be built through motor manipulation which will encourage exploration of space and time, factors necessary to the development of concepts of motion and form. This, as we have mentioned over and over again, is a basic foundation for all children, but especially for all exceptional children.* The blind child needs the boxes, and the balls, and the cups, and all sorts of stuff, presented in a meaningful way that it might encourage rather than overwhelm him.

Tactile sensitivity is an open door for the blind child in art. Lines may be found to move and produce shapes. Textured surfaces may define forms. Collage experiences may be used to not only help the child discern form and enrich his concepts, but to develop his total gestalt capabilities; his aesthetic sensitivities, as well. He may start with just a single length of yarn and a piece of cardboard and gradually build up to a multitude of materials and forms. He may be encouraged to develop "feeling boxes" through which one may walk by use of the fingers. Almost any art material, aside from paint, may be used successfully with blind children if we remember their few basic needs and aid them in responding with those needs in mind. Even crayon on rough paper towels may be felt by the blind child who has a keener and deeper discernment in tactual experiencing than we ourselves possess.

While we have been speaking generally of the congenitally blind child, some attention should be given to the child who loses vision partially and at a later age. Little difference in the process of perceptual experiencing is noticed with such individuals. Lowenfeld carefully noted, however, that as a rule the visually-minded child will benefit by any remnants of vision that he may have, while the haptic-minded child will be hampered by such capability to see. In figure 118 we see a crayon drawing by Carol, a partially-sighted girl of eleven years of age. Carol drew herself with a friend having a root beer at the drug store. Her visually-minded perceptual process is evident in the spatial depth and general realism of the drawing. Yet she took over a week to draw the picture and held her face almost to the paper as she drew.

The Child with an Auditory Impairment

Like the child with a vision impairment, the child with a hearing impairment may be handicapped, to varying degrees, by the loss of function. Identifying with the experiencing of the child is again the first step in recognizing his needs and in devising strategies for helping him develop. Emotional detachment caused by a lack of environmental awareness and interaction is usually the deaf child's greatest difficulty and the factor we can help him resolve through art. There is little art could offer in regard to the actual hearing loss.

If we firmly hold our hands completely over our ears, we will immediately recognize the detachment that the deaf child feels. *He does not totally experience his environment at one time.* A good one-half to two-thirds of his environ-

Figure 118. "Having a Root
Beer" by Carol, 11 years.

ment is always hidden from his awareness. This is an extreme impairment when
we recognize how important it is to constantly experience one's self in the spatial
environment. From this fact we note that the deaf child will, as a rule, experience some difficulty in orienting his body to space and time. He will, as a result,
lack meaning in the body reference and have trouble to some degree in discerning motion and form. He will also lack meaning in verbal communication and
thus tend to suffer with strong emotions for which he lacks an adequate means
of expression. He is far more prone to emotional disturbance than the blind child
and is usually considered more seriously handicapped.

The drawing and painting expression of the deaf child often indicates his
feeling of isolation. In figure 119 Charles painted himself talking with his hands.
We would expect the exaggerated character of the arms from the type of subject. Notice, however, the heavy black line about the head which suggests his
"bound in" self. It almost appears that the personality has been pushed into

Figure 119. "Talking" by Charles,
8 years.

a can. Very often, as in his painting, the head is drawn extra large. It seems to be an emphasis upon the self-entity ego-circle.

In the work of Harry (fig. 120), a boy of eleven years with total loss of hearing in one ear, we notice a strong feeling of isolation. He was in the same class as Carol (fig. 118) and also was responding to the motivation concerning a root beer with a friend in the drug store. Everyone at the counter sits stiffly and separately apart. There is no expression indicating conversation as in Carol's drawing.

Figure 120. "Having a Root Beer" by Harry, 11 years.

Deaf children need the physical games in the early years which would enable them to better identify and interact in the world of space and motion. They need to be drawn out emotionally to "unload" their feelings in art—feelings which are not verbalized. Three-dimensional activity such as modeling or carving should be encouraged. Motivating them is extremely difficult as they cannot communicate verbally at an early age. Perhaps the best means is dramatization or actual participation in an experience with rapid opportunity for expression in art made immediately available afterward.

REFERENCES

BENDER, LAURETTA. *Child Psychiatric Techniques.* Springfield, Ill.: Charles C Thomas, Publisher, 1952.

———— "Post-Encephalitic Behavior Disorders in Childhood." *Encephalitis, A Clinical Study,* edited by Josephine Neal. New York: Grune and Stratton, Inc., 1943.

———— "The Goodenough Test in Chronic Encephalitis in Children." *J. Nervous and Mental Diseases 91* (1940): 277-286.

———— "The Psychological Problems of Children with Organic Brain Disorders." *American Journal of Orthopsychiatry 19* (1949): 404-415.

———— and SILVER, A. "Body-Image Problems of the Brain-Damaged Child." *Journal of Social Issues 4* (1948): 84-89.

BUCK, JOHN. *The H-T-P Technique: Qualitative and Quantitative Scoring Manual.* Monograph of *J. of Clinical Psychology,* October 1948.

CENTERS, L., and CENTERS, R. "A Comparison of the Body-Images of Amputee and Non-Amputee Children as Revealed in Figure Drawings." *Journal of Projective Techniques* 27 (1963): 158-165.

COHN, R. *The Person Symbol in Clinical Medicine.* Springfield, Ill.: Charles C Thomas, Publisher, 1960.

FLORES, A. "Two-Dimensional Art for the Blind." Unpublished master's thesis, Sacramento State College, 1968.

GOLDSTEIN, K. *After-Effects of Brain-Injuries in War.* New York: Grune and Stratton, Inc., 1942.

HAMMER, E. *The H-T-P Clinical Research Manual.* Beverly Hills, Calif.: Western Psychological Services, 1955.

HANVIK, LEO. et al. "Diagnosis of Cerebral Dysfunction in Child." *American Journal of Diseases of Children 101* (1961): 364-375.

—— and ANDERSON, A. "The Effect of Focal Brain Lesions on Recall and the Production of Rotations in the Bender Gestalt Test." *Journal of Consulting Psychology* 14 (1950): 197-198.

HEAD, H. *Aphasia and Kindred Disorders of Speech.* New York: Hafner Publishing Co., Inc., 1963.

HEBB, D. "The Effect of Early and Late Brain Injury upon the Test Scores, and the Nature of Adult Intelligence." *Proc. of the Am. Philosophical Society 85* (1942): 275-292.

JOLLES, I. *A Catalogue for the Qualitative Interpretation of the House-Tree-Person.* Beverly Hills, Calif.: Western Psychological Services, 1964.

LEHTINEN, LAURA. *Have You Ever Known a Perceptually Handicapped Child?* Los Angeles Chapter of the California Association for Neurologically Handicapped Children, P.O. Box 604, Los Angeles, Calif. 90053.

LOWENFELD, VIKTOR. *Creative and Mental Growth.* New York: The Macmillan Co., 1947.

MARTORANA, A. "A Comparison of the Personal, Emotional, and Family Adjustments of Crippled and Normal Children." Unpublished doctoral theses, University of Minnesota, 1954.

MICHAL-SMITH, H. "Identification of Pathological Cerebral Function Through the H-T-P Technique." *Journal of Clinical Psychology, 9* (1953): 293-295.

PFISTER, H. "Farbe und Bewegung in der Zeichnung Geisterkranker." *Schweiz Arch. Neurol. and Psychiat. 34* (1934): 325-365.

REZNIKOFF, M., and TOMBLEN, D. "The Use of Human Figure Drawings in the Diagnosis of Organic Pathology." *Journal of Psychology 20* (1956): 467-470.

RUBEN, E. "Synsopleuede Figurer." *Principles of Gestalt Psychology.* Copenhagen, 1915 (English Ed.: N. Y.: Harcourt and Brace, 1935).

STRAUSS, A., and WERNER, H. "Disorders of Conceptual Thinking in the Brain-Injured Child." *Journal of Nervous and Mental Diseases 96* (1942): 153-172.

STRAUSS, A., and LEHTINEN, L. *Psychopathology and Education of the Brain-Injured Child.* New York: Grune and Stratton, Inc., 1947.

STRAUSS, A., and KEPHART, N. *Psychopathology and Education of the Brain-Injured Child. Vol. 2.* New York: Grune and Stratton, Inc., 1955.

UHLIN, D., and DICKSON, J. "The Effect of Figure-Ground Reversal in the H-T-P Drawings by Spastic Cerebral Palsied Children." *Journal of Clinical Psychology 26* (1970): 87-88.

UHLIN, D. "The Basis of Art for Neurologically Handicapped Children." *Psychiatry and Art Vol. 2: Art Interpretation and Art Therapy*, I. Jakab, ed. Basel/N. Y.: S. Karger Co., 1969.

VERNIER, C. *Projective Test Productions: I. Projective Drawings.* New York: Grune and Stratton, Inc., 1952.

WERNER, H., and THUMA, B. "A Deficiency in the Perception of Apparent Motion in Children with Brain-Injury." *American Journal of Psychology 55* (1942): 58-67.

—— "Critical Flicker-Frequency in Children with Brain-Injury. *American Journal of Psychology 55* (1942): 394-399.

WERNER, H., and STRAUSS, A. "Pathology of Figure-Background Relation in the Child." *Journal of Abnormal and Social Psychology 36* (1941): 236-248.

—— "Types of Visuo-Motor Activity in Their Relation to Low and High Performance Ages." *American Journal of Mental Deficiency 44* (1939): 163-168.

5 Art and the Emotionally Disturbed Child

We have previously concerned ourselves, in our discussion of the exceptional child, with those impairments which have a basic organic character. Now our attention must focus upon those children whose impairment has the basic character of a psychical disturbance. We will note that this type of impairment is first of all difficult to recognize and then difficult to classify. One factor which often contributes to such difficulty is a deeper organic etiology. In the next chapter just such a case will be discussed. Here we will concern ourselves with impairments which, from all study, appear to have a purely *functional* origin. Our considerations will therefore be primarily from a psychoanalytic viewpoint.

Functional disturbances arise from a distortion of communication within the apperceptive process. The emotional identification of the child, for the acceptance of communicated reality, may become an extremely difficult task, and rejection may occur even from the earliest beginnings of life. Breakdown may also come gradually after reality structuring has once begun. Since the emotions interact with the rational functioning of the individual, when breakdown does occur, the mind will also function in a distorted manner, and as a result, the individual becomes both emotionally and rationally detached or disassociated from reality. This may occur to varying degrees of severity at various intervals of time. The younger the child when disturbance forms, the more constant and powerful will be the effect of the impairment on his behavior. He may become highly autonomous from reality, and the term *autistic* is therefore often a very appropriate label. Kanner (1966) uses the term *infantile autism* for the severely disturbed child who, from earliest life, is apart from reality. Behaviorally such a child may be very passive and "in his own world" most of the time, but he also contains the potential for violence and aggression in overacting to outside stimuli. Behaviorally he may be bizarre and do highly unusual things such as eat crayons or dirt with no apparent distaste. Many emotionally disturbed children move in stereotyped physical motor patterns as evidenced in continuous rocking or whirling, and they may even become fascinated by bright spinning forms that make noise. At times the vortical motion appears almost to be symbolic of the abyss in which they live, but more accurately it probably indicates to us the loss of space-time orientation which normal children experience through bodily kinesthesis.

When we deal with a disturbed child, the parents are of particular concern, for they very basically are the most important factor in the reality which the child finds unacceptable. Needless to say, many children ambulate along through their childhood years and then suffer a major shattering in their late teens when they are faced with the prospects of advanced education, jobs, marriage, and military service. The adult schizophrenic may often be evidenced as a personality which has ambulated from childhood on the emotional level of early childhood.

It is imperative for the mental-emotional health of the growing child that we detect and treat abnormal psychic tendencies and the etiological factors which cause such disturbance. Art is an excellent reflective tool for this purpose, for in the art process the individual continues to express and grapple with unconscious psychic turmoil even when severely disturbed. Through the language of the symbol he will communicate to us and reach out for our understanding and help. The symbol alone will enable us to differentiate emotional disturbance from neurological handicap and mental deficiency.

We will attempt initially to offer some clarification of the etiology of emotional disturbance in the child and then view typical behavioral characteristics in the child's art. Finally, we will note strategy for psychotherapy of the child through his art.

Etiology of Emotional Disturbance in the Child

Children need affection for the nourishment of their emotions just as they need physical food for the sustenance of their bodies. Without love the real human personality is never born. Rothenberg (1960) writes of "Johnny" who lived in an incubator the first few months of his life and who, as a result, failed to enter into human contact and response. We must never assume that physical birth and growth will be paralleled with psychic birth and growth. The emotionally disturbed child is often found to be detached from reality almost from the moment of birth, and therefore he cannot truly be called "schizophrenic." That is to say, since he may never have entered into a reality structuring of any extent, we cannot really say he is "split" from reality in the typical schizophrenic sense. In recognizing the severity of such a condition, we note that he must then "relive" or begin at the initial phases of life and grow emotionally from the point where his emotions could not accept the real environment. Other disturbed children may be less severely involved and may be lacking, to some degree, a successful resolving of basic life tasks in early childhood. This latter type of child is the individual who often ambulates for many years and is difficult to detect.

Most writers, such as Frankenstein (1959), recognize the early years as the more formative period of personality, and they therefore emphasize the mother-child relationship. Frankenstein suggests that psychopathic etiology may be found in:

1. More or less complete lack of maternal contact and care.
2. Indolence and apathy in the mother's attitude toward the child.
3. Overt rejection of the child by the mother.
4. Sudden disappearance of the mother.
5. Maternal indulgence.

It is interesting to note that the first four criteria indicate a lack of affection derived from the mother. We know, from our discussion of the normal child, that self-identification must come first *in* and *through* the mother image. The fifth criterion in an indirect manner also suggests a lack of love, since most writers, like Levy (1943), agree that overprotection and absorption of the child's personality by the mother is simply another form of rejection. Such indulgence is actually found to be a compensation for guilt experienced by the parent.

In discussing the normal child we noted the typical developmental tasks of the young child in the drawing of the circle, the cross, and the rectangle. When used symbolically, such reference to form in drawing provides us not only with a basis for recognition of the level of emotional disturbance, but with some understanding of basic etiology as well. We may state: *If the child is arrested emotionally with a basic life task unresolved, then he will continue to project his struggle with that problem through predominant forms or subjects which symbolize that level of conflict in early childhood.* A child of ten years may thus be found fixed in the production of circular forms, or other symbolical references, which would indicate his struggle to identify as a physical self-entity apart from, but emotionally dependent upon, the mother. An older child may tend to be preoccupied with the symmetry of the cross form, or other sexually paradoxical images, and thereby indicate his continued and confused attempt to resolve a sexual-self role which normally would take place at three to four years of age. Finally, a child may continue to struggle with the problem of ego-closure far beyond the age of four to seven years and thus project his difficulty in the rectangular "grid" form, or other significant overdetailing and structuring of forms.

While this theoretical construction tends to oversimplify the basis for the identification of the disturbed child, it provides a reference from which we might examine more closely the individual child and his particular impairment, especially in relation to his home environment.

Emotional Disturbance and Art Expression

The symbolical significance of form and the use of subject in a symbolic manner both provide a basis for understanding the art of the disturbed child. We will discuss these manifestations in the art of disturbed cases primarily with reference to etiology evidenced in form symbolism.

The Circle

We have noted earlier how the circle represents the child bound up emotionally in the mother. What will occur when the relationship of the child to the mother fails to be established, is impaired by separation, or the emotional climate established by the mother is one of indifference and rejection? We may simply state that the child in such a case will desperately attempt to identify with the mother, even if it means a return to the security of the circular context of the womb which, after all, did offer a type of perfect security. The closeness of the relationship was broken only by birth. In figures 121, 122, and 123 we note the work of Mickie, whose art for some time was as much an enigma as he himself. An Rh_o factor was the only suspect basis for his impairment.

In figure 121 we see a typical drawing by Mickie at six years of age and in figure 122 a similar "man" drawn by Mickie at ten years of age. A sudden revelation came one day when he drew figure 123 with white crayon on black paper. There is an emphasis upon the circular form, and an unmistakable fetal image appears in the mouth of the "face." It is obvious that Mickie is identifying as a fetal child within the mother. At ten years of age this is Mickie's level of emotional identification.

Repetition of the circular form will appear in many subjects drawn by emotionally disturbed children. Ricky (figs. 124 and 125) was fascinated by spinning objects and often drew airplanes with a dozen or more propellers. His human figures were people with "empty" tubelike bodies and highly stylized heads which contain the same circular repetition in the ears. Schilder (1950) has noted that any hole in the body is easily symbolized in other holes of the same human figure. The roundness of the head, the eyes, the ears, the mouth, the umbilicus, the anus, and so on—all become possible symbols of autism in the child. While the circle is the simplest gestalt form and suggests the egocentricity of autism from a lack of motor reference in time and space, it remains, as well, a symbol of the child bound up in the mother.

above: **Figure 121.**   Drawing by Mickie, 6 years

above right: **Figure 122.**   "Man" by Mickie, 10 years.

right: **Figure 123.**   Drawing by Mickie, 10 years

Figure 124. "Airplane" by Ricky, 10 years.

Figure 125. "Family" by Ricky, 10 years

A quiet boy of fifteen drew figures 126 and 127. The emphasis is upon circular form with concentric repetition. He is very passive but can become extremely violent at times as is evidenced in the horns in figure 127. The mouth is open or absent, there is an emphasis upon the buttons as a dependency form, and the arms are weak or absent indicating a feeling of helplessness.

Self-destruction or nihilism suggested for one's self may be an overture of escape and despair evidenced in drawings. Running away, drug abuse, suicide attempts, and other similar behavioral manifestations are often the older child's expression which parallels holding one's breath or hiding in early childhood. In figure 128 we see the drawing of a person by a ten-year-old boy who runs away often. The head is simply a drop of paint. There are no hands or feet, and this indicates his helplessness and lack of security. The color is that of a bruise —black, blue, and purple. He is emotionally "wounded" and calls for affection by his act of running away. The comment of his parents when he is found by the police is "Let him stay in the juvenile center for a few days. That will teach him a lesson."

Figure 126.   Self-image by boy 15 years

Figure 127.   Self-image by boy 15 years

Figure 128.   Figure by runaway boy 10 years.

A girl, twenty-six years old, drew figures 129 and 130. She had been taking heavy doses of amphetamines and LSD and was just starting on heroin. She drew these people and then said, "They are like butterflies without wings—trapped like me." Here the same concentric form persists as a symbol of autism or escape. Like most severely impaired and disturbed individuals, she emphasizes the head and almost totally neglects the body, which symbolically is cut off or empty. The experiencing of the body is simply not accepted psychically. Often even the face, as the face of the cat in *Alice's Adventures in Wonderland*, finally disappears—perhaps until only the smile, or less, is left.

Figure 129. Self-image by female 26 years (during withdrawal from drug abuse).

Figure 130. Self-image by female 26 years (during withdrawal after drug abuse).

The extreme detachment made in late adolescence, or even in adult life, is often gradually formed from its origin in early childhood. In figure 131 we see a ceramic figure made by an eighteen-year-old institutionalized boy. He has regressed to the state of an infant and, except for the hollow form of the torso, looks like a bird opening his mouth just above the edge of the nest, as if waiting for the nourishment suggested in the mother's return.

Figure 131. Ceramic figure by institutionalized male 18 years

In figures 132, 133, and 134 we see the drawings of George who is now in his late forties. His parents both died when he was two or three years of age. He was moved from one orphanage to another and was in and out of many foster homes. As a young man he joined the army and made it his career. In essence, the army became the mother for him and maintained him for a number of years. He was clothed, fed, given work, and had a friend or two. At present he still reacts on a primitive level, and his human figure concepts indicate the emptiness of his felt identity. In figure 132 his childlike dependency within the context of the magic feminine circle clearly reveals his emotional level.

Figure 132. Self figure by George, 46 years

Figure 133. Self figure by George, 42 years

Figure 134. Self figure by George, 42 years

The Cross

The cross form, as we have seen in previous discussion, represents the dichotomy or dilemma of the child as he seeks to resolve the question of a self-sex role at three to four years of age. His models for the masculine and feminine roles are his parents. If they play their roles well, we can expect the child to form a clear identification within the scope of the home, which will equip him for adequate participation later in a larger society. On the other hand, a poor parental model, a missing parental model, or an absorbing or rejecting parent may cause great confusion for the child.

One particular danger always presents itself in the parent-child relationship at this age. While it is normally resolved as a rule in most homes, it becomes a major basis for emotional disturbance where unusual circumstances compound the problem. It is essentially that the child will tend to gravitate in an almost "romantic" manner toward the parent of the opposite sex and then, to some degree, consider the parent of like sex to be a rival. The little girl plays the mother's role by taking care of the "baby"; she gives tea parties and begins to pattern herself after the mother as we would anticipate. Also, however, in this paradox of what Freud called an "Oedipus complex," she loves the father and seeks his affection, while at the same time she rejects the mother. She may even wish the mother would die, as the little girl of three years, who drew a house for daddy, a house for baby, a house for brother, and a house for herself. When asked where mother's house was she replied, "Mommy's house died." The mother had to be reassured that all was "normal." If the father takes advantage of the girl's attention and in turn overly responds to her advances, she may tend to identify too thoroughly in and through the father, and the dilemma of sexual identification may be prolonged and perhaps never resolved. The same circumstance may be presented to the mother and her son, especially if the mother fulfills her need for romantic affection in the boy. The stage is usually set by incompatibility, separation, or divorce of the parents. The child who is overabsorbed by the parent may become inverted in sexual identification, or he may find it necessary to overcompensate in his proper sexual role, due to a threatening unconscious which carries with itself the contrasexual image. In short, the child may become a sexual invert or a paranoid reactor. Such a dilemma may easily form the basis of severe psychic turmoil, and behavior may become that of the typical sociopath. Many criminal types may be traced to the confusion just mentioned as evidenced in their childhood years. Because masculine behavior is usually overt in character, the man projects his hostility and aggression outward toward others and thereby terminates himself in prison. The woman most often projects her hostility inward and thus terminates her life in a state hospital.

While the roots of the sexual dilemma are found early in the life of the individual, the expression of the paradoxical feelings is not usually seen clearly in art until seven or eight years when sexual symbols are first dynamically expressed. In figure 135 a nine-year-old boy drew a type of self-image with the following story on the back:

> A man was on a deserted island and the sharks were after him. He bombed the sharks but demolished the island. Now the man will fall and will be eaten by the sharks.

Notice the symmetry of the cross in the composition of the drawing. It speaks of the ambivalency of identity that he feels. The man has his secure footing on the ground—a symbol of the mother. It is always the unconscious feminine "mother" which threatens the man, but he will usually project that threat in such a manner that it appears from outside. It is by reacting to a threat from outside, which he actually may create, that he destroys the "woman" that threatens him, along with himself. Thus we see that ancient paradoxical process which is typical of the paranoid reactor. Here is the compensating male who, like Hitler, thought he could only be secure when all things were subordinated to himself. Yet the threat was at once arising and pushing from within. It has been said that behind every successful man there is a woman, but it is clear here that the "woman" may work from within.

Figure 135. "Man on a Deserted Island" by boy 9 years

In figure 136 we note a ten-year-old boy's drawing of a strong man. It is an obvious self-image. The mountains rising in the background suggest the dominant mother. The overlapping of the mountains indicates his extroversion and field-dependency which Witkin (1954) notes lies in a "growth-constricting" mother. The large belt buckle reveals a strong umbilical tie, and even though the man is strong in biceps, he also has strong feminine characteristics as are displayed in the ballet-type shoes, the breastlike development of the pectoral muscles, and the cleft in the chin which is a vaginal symbol on the "torso" of the face. The body position is arrowlike as if to indicate his desire to rise above the mother-image of the mountain. Figure 137 is very similar but from an older boy in a penal facility.

Figure 136. "Strongman" by boy 10 years

Figure 137. Self-image by boy 17 years

Girls experience similar distortions of identity which place them, too, in a paradox of sexual dilemma. In figures 138, 139, 140, and 141 we find a H-T-P series from a sixteen-year-old girl. The house (fig. 138) has been badly abused as a symbol of her aggression toward the mother. From the tree (fig. 139) hangs a feminine circle which has been stabbed and punctured by nails. The human figures (figs. 140 and 141) clearly indicate her own glamorous but masculine self and her superiority over men.

Figure 138.   House by girl 16 years

Figure 139.   Tree by girl 16 years

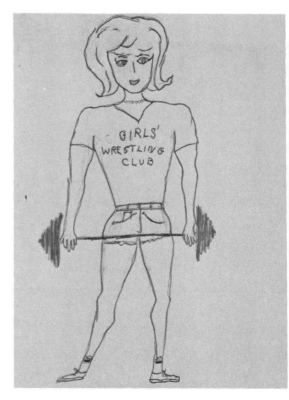

Figure 140.   Man by girl 16 years

Figure 141.   Girl by girl 16 years

Raymond (figs. 142 and 143) is a ten-year-old boy who was referred by his mother for evaluation. When he arrived, it was obvious that his behavior was highly unusual and that he was greatly suffering with psychic pain. He could not sit still, his head moved with mechanical tics, and he periodically made a bizarre noise. His self-projection (fig. 142) contains a large head (egocentricity), a long neck (rejection of bodily identity), legs moving directly to the belt (lack of sexual acceptance), and peculiar "cuts" on the nose, arms, and neck. In the interview he mentioned his desire to cut his fingers with razor blades. Such a symbol in drawing suggests a self-castration. In his family drawing (fig. 143) he draws the self image below the emphasized figure of his mother. It is obvious that he is preoccupied with her person. The father and older brother appear to the right side of the paper. When we spoke with Raymond, he mentioned a dream in which he drove a car into a swimming pool and was thus unable to breathe. The feeling of rejection for, and detachment from, his body was symbolically expressed. Then he later mentioned a dream in which he entered his mother's bedroom at night and her bed was "way down there, and my thumb was stiff." An erection of the phallus in his desire for the mother was thereby indicated. Further study and interview of the parents disclosed that they were incompatible, and they were subsequently divorced two years later. At that time Raymond stayed with his mother, and the older brother went to live with father. The mother had derived needed affection from Raymond and, in effect, had seduced him. He would now carry the suffering of guilt experienced from the relationship.

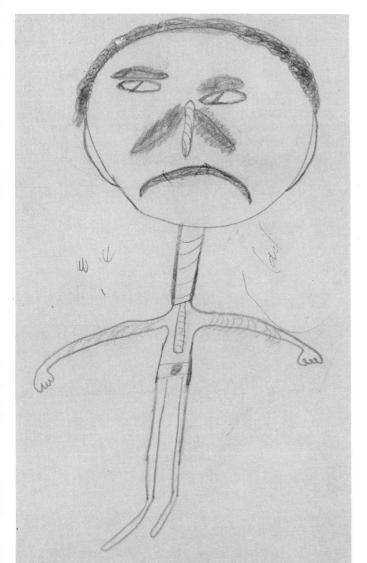

left: **Figure 142.**   Self by Raymond, 10 years

below: **Figure 143.**   Family by Raymond, 10 years

Long necks and birdlike creatures often are symbolical of the effeminate-male personality. In figures 144 and 145 we see such images in drawings by Chuck, a sixteen-year-old paranoid schizophrenic youth. We notice that the dinosaur even has breasts. This case, reported by Crowl (1968), became obvious when he was asked to draw the most "unpleasant concept" and he responded by drawing figure 146 with the comment, "Father has just shot my lizard." It again is clear in such imagery that the parent had destroyed the path of identification which would allow the child to normally develop. The father, in this case, has actually destroyed the boy's opportunity of sexual identification with himself as symbolically portrayed in the dead phallic "lizard." The mother had deserted the family.

Figure 144. Bird by Chuck, 16 years

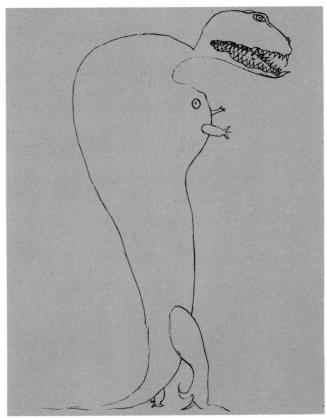

Figure 145. Dinosaur by Chuck, 16 years

Figure 146. "Father Shot My Lizard" by Chuck, 16 years.

Even if the individual ambulates along psychically under the typical circumstances which we have discussed, he will feel incompetent and find it necessary to obtain the masculine power he so desperately needs. A forger often reveals such a dilemma in H-T-P drawings (figs. 147, 148, and 149). The house drawing (fig. 147) indicates the strength of the mother and the subject's involvement with her. Even the driveway penetrates the house as a symbolic sexual relationship. The person and tree (figs. 148 and 149) indicate the weakness and depression of the subject. In an overlay of the person and tree drawings, the broken branch perfectly overlays with the neck, revealing the suicidal tendencies within

Figure 147.   House by Forger, 21 years

Figure 148.   Person by Forger, 21 years

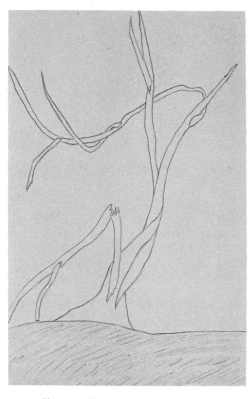

Figure 149.   Tree by Forger, 21 years

this young man. Though he is twenty-one years of age, his present difficulties originated very early in life through the parent-child relationship.

Rabbits, birds, and other small, timid creatures are often the projected self-identity of the male who is weak or sexually-inverted. They may turn to deviate sexual patterns of behavior such as exhibitionism and voyeurism, or possibly to more overt homosexuality. The popularity of latent homosexual publications and entertainment indicates the magnitude of the problem today. Some individuals, through their self-identification in the dilemma, edit highly successful magazines and fly around the world like big "bunnies" in their personal "birds." In figures 150-154 we note the drawings of Bing, a boy of thirteen years, who identifies as an emasculated bird and other similar weak and timid creatures. The cold, sharp ground usually looms up above him or completely surrounds him as he shakes in a homosexual panic (fig. 154) as "batman."

Figure 150.   Drawing by Bing, 13 years

Figure 151.   Drawing by Bing, 13 years

Figure 152. Drawing by Bing, 13 years

Figure 153. Drawing by Bing, 13 years

Figure 154. Drawing by Bing, 13 years

Some people, today, do not believe that the homosexual is a threat to himself or society, but most of the evidence is strongly to the contrary. Any individual who finds it difficult to identify within the context of normal culture will aggressively seek to change that society or withdraw from it. In figures 155 and 156 we note human figure drawings by Carl, a sixteen-year-old boy. He is an overt homosexual and had just been removed from his local high school. Notice the exhibiting of the phallic tongue, the lack of nose, and the vaginal character of the ear in figure 155. In figure 156 we find no hands or feet, and the hard, shell-like concentric barriers of the body, along with the "rat-fink" label, reveal his essential nihilism and despair. The degree of disturbance at this point was just beginning to surface after exposure and expulsion.

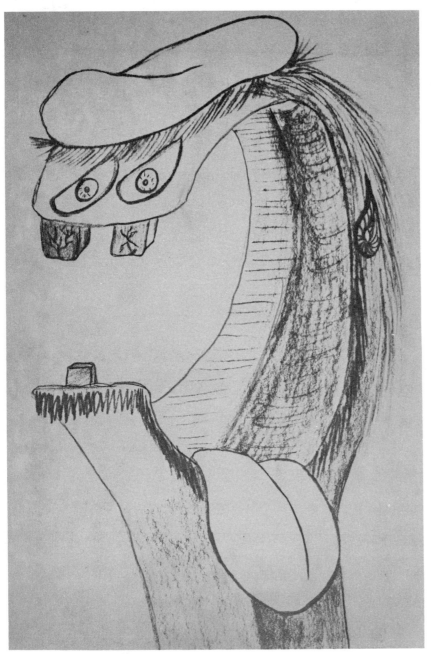

Figure 155. Self-image by Carl, 16 years

Figure 156. Self-image by Carl, 16 years

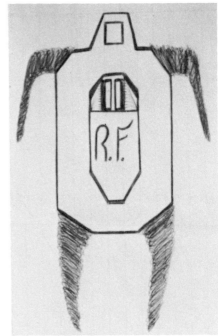

Three juvenile sex offenders reveal their crimes in the ceramic images of figures 157, 158, and 159. The smooth surface, preoccupation with "holes" in the facial "body," and the weak chin with a vaginal cleft—all indicate overt homosexuality in figure 157. The hostile horns, the lack of eyes (lack of self-acceptance of actions), and the protruding tongue reveal exhibitionism in figure 158. Figure 159 was produced by a rapist, and he reveals himself in knifelike teeth, a strong jaw, and protruding eyes. In criminal sexual acts the offender projects and destroys the feminine image over which he often feels he must exercise power. Aggressive acts and suicidal acts have much in common, and it is not surprising to find homicide followed by suicide.

above: **Figure 157.** Homosexual image

above right: **Figure 158.** Exhibitionist image

right: **Figure 159.** Rapist image

Figure 160.   Image of sexual aggression, juvenile boy 16 years

In figure 160 we note again the dangerousness of the juvenile who is threatened by his feminine unconscious self. The feminine circle is jabbed over and over again.

The Rectangle

When one's environmental perspective fails to provide an acceptable climate for the structuring and maintenance of reality, desperate attempts are made to organize and subordinate that environment which poses a threat. If such efforts fail, there is no recourse but to withdraw into the reference of the body-self and then finally out into the transcendental world of the spirit where space and time cease to exist. Disassociation is a frightening experience, for no child or adult ever leaves reality on the basis of his own desire. It is the purest form of existentialism, and the journey is a house of horrors where motion factors are fragmented and the real events of the temporal world gradually become more unreal and crystalline. It is of our interest here to consider in art expression the dissolution of the ego of the child as he experiences a breakdown of identity within his environment, and then with his own body. In most respects such a process is the reverse of normal personality growth. The structured detailing of rectangular organization is our basic reference for ego-structuring, and therefore we may expect a preoccupation and struggle within the context of that form.

Many factors previously mentioned may contribute to a difficulty in identifying with one's self in the context of the real environment. The child may suffer the loss of the mother's affection, and this may have a severe effect if she had previously been overprotective and affectionate. In figures 161, 162, and 163 we see drawings by Mike, a boy of eight years who had been the sole recipient of his mother's affection all the years of his young life. He has identified in her person to the degree that he lacks a strong self-identification. Now he has been "replaced" by a baby sister whom he draws in figure 161. He not only would like to wipe out the sister, but in his jealousy he would like to be the sister, for his own identity is feminine to begin with. Here we notice the concentric circular forms again in the ears, a preoccupation with the eyelashes, the dependency buttons down the front of the dress, a tremendous structuring of the teeth, and sharp hostile fingers on the hands. Mike is obviously a very

Figure 161. "That's My Sister" by Mike, 8 years.

intelligent boy, but also a very disturbed boy. In figure 162 we note that the whole drawing takes on the character of a large face. The suns are simply eyes, again with lashes, and even each "eye" in itself has a face with eyelashes included. The tree is highly detailed or "structured" in the upper region and thus is an expression of his rational preoccupation. The trunk of the tree is a single line which speaks of a loss of bodily self and a very weak emotional "footing." In figure 162, he replaced his bird subjects with a rabbit. In telling about his tree drawing, he said, "That's the bunny rabbit and he jumped, and jumped, and jumped until he bumped his head on the tree. He cried and cried and ran home to tell his mama." Mike is desperate for attention of any type, positive or negative, for it in some degree substitutes for the loss of his mother's affection.

Figure 162.   Drawing   by   Mike, 8 years.

Figure 163.   Tree   drawing   by Mike, 8 years.

Other factors which we have not examined may also contribute to the difficulty the child experiences in ego-structuring. In figure 164 we find the work of Henry, a seven-year-old black boy who lives in an all-white neighborhood and attends an all-white school. When he drew this picture of his family, he left his face off and thus indicated his lack of self-acceptance. He is certainly not emotionally disturbed at this point, but such a circumstance of difference in race, physical appearance, cultural background, and similar factors could compound a child's attempts in structuring and maintaining reality, especially if the home were not ideal as in Henry's case.

Figure 164. Family by Henry, 7 years.

Children who are confused in regard to the reality about themselves are often highly threatened by the rules and demands of others. It is not unusual to find them moving rapidly out of a very passive state into violent behavior. Teachers of the exceptional sometimes make such statements as, "We are just going to have to do something about Jimmy as he is beginning to kick and bite the other children." Well, great! It looks as though Jimmy is improving! We must keep in mind that interaction with the environment, even in a hostile behavior, is far healthier than withdrawal. Disturbed children will usually come out fighting, and we had best let them win a few even if it means shin guards and helmets. If we force them back into their shell, we will make it twice as difficult to encounter reality again. It will be well to look carefully at their deeper difficulties.

In figure 165, Penny, a seven-year-old girl in a "slow" second-grade class, has drawn a self-image. The arms have the appearance of paper ribbons with no hands. Her helpless feeling is evident. In testing, her verbal intelligence was measured at an IQ of 86 while her performance record revealed an IQ of 126. After drawing the self-image, she jabbed at it over and over again as if attacking herself.

Figure 165. Person by Penny, 7 years.

What could best be called "barriers" or "fences" are often in evidence as a protective device for the body-self. It is as if the child has crawled into a box to protect himself from a hostile environment. In figures 166 and 167 we note such protective forms in the work of Arthur, a seven-year-old who was being evaluated. His color usage was also highly unusual—green features and an orange, purple, and blue body. There was a definite feeling of the body being "cut-up" or segmented by the color. His ground color was never green—always orange, black, or purple. The symmetry of the drawings and the preference for these particular colors suggest a paranoid reactor. Purple especially may be evidenced as a color of sexual dilemma—masculine red mixed with feminine blue.

above: **Figure 166.** Person by Arthur, 7 years.

right: **Figure 167.** House by Arthur, 7 years.

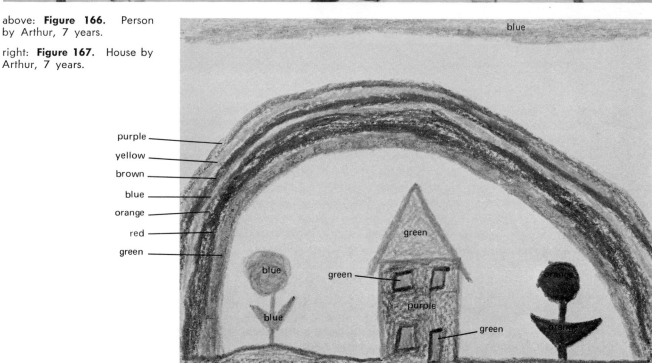

A boy in much the same condition is Irving (fig. 168) who is sixteen years old and is presently detained in a penal facility. His drawing is highly structured and detailed. Defensiveness is the chief characteristic. The elevated "mountain-like" domes and the symmetry of the cross form indicate, also, a paranoid reactor. He may be expected to behave in strong, passive-aggressive extremes.

Figure 168.   House by Irving, 16 years

Dwight, another boy in the same institution (fig. 169), is pre-occupied with the same symmetry. He very carefully structured his ceramic figure with small detailed dots. He counted them over and over again to make certain that both sides were even in number. There are no eyes to the figure, and the back of the head has been cut off.

Drug abuse tends to fragment the individual from reality in much the same manner as emotional disturbance. In figures 170-173 we note how Christine, an eighteen-year-old girl, struggled to organize the chaotic perceptions of her environment into real form. Over several weeks' time, she moved from the disorganization of figures 170 and 171, to a type of pointilism (fig. 172), and finally to a realistic ability (fig. 173).

Figure 169.   Ceramic bust by Dwight, 16 years.

Figure 170. Drawing by Christine, 18 years.

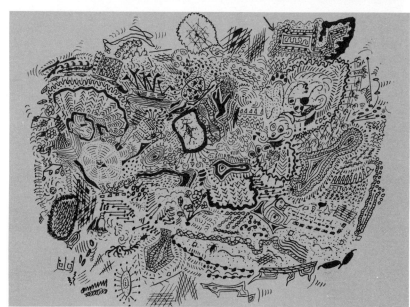

Figure 171. Drawing by Christine, 18 years

Figure 172. Houses by Christine, 18 years

Figure 173. Pots by Christine, 18 years

When the individual withdraws from a threatening environment, he will, as a rule, draw only the bodily reference, and if his condition continues to deteriorate, he will lose a sensitivity to the body as well. This is often evidenced by an attack upon the human form and then a projection of an "empty" or segmented form. Actual detachment may occur through some type of severing at the neck; this is frequently indicative that the individual is living in the psyche (head) and is disregarding sensory communication (hollow body). The head in such a case is often highly detailed and rigidly stylized.

In figure 174 a boy of thirteen tears apart the bodily self. It is hung, electrocuted, and shot at by both cannon and bullet. Notice also the weak and ineffective hands. He drew three similar human figures over a year's time. The following years he attended school less and less until he dropped out completely when he was sixteen.

Figure 174. "Myself" by Tim, 13 years.

Figure 175 is drawn by a ten-year-old boy. Here we notice a fine break at the neck. The stylized head is much like a cork that does not quite reach the neck of the empty bodily form. The only detail on the body is a belt buckle without even a belt attached to it. Here again we see the concentric linear forms in the ears. The figure is rigidly symmetrical; even the nose is split down the center. The boy was a very withdrawn paranoid reactor.

Melvin, a nine-year-old boy, drew the human images in figures 176 and 177. He is so dissociated from bodily identity in figure 176 that he is not even certain regarding the number or position of the limbs. In figure 177 he drew a segmented human, and far up in the right corner of the paper is a small dark-red sun which suggests his dogmatic and rejecting father.

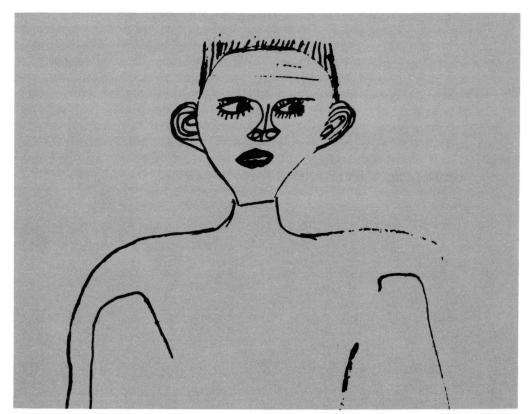

Figure 175. Person by James, 10 years. [Lines darkened]

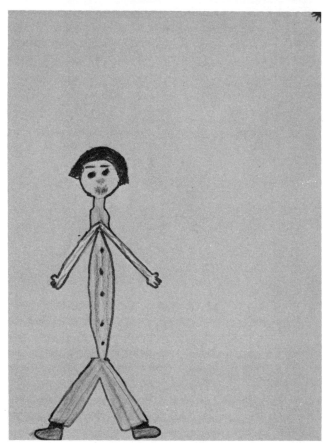

Figure 176. Person by Melvin, 9 years

Figure 177. Person by Melvin, 9 years

Paula, a sixteen-year-old girl, drew the H-T-P series in figures 178-181. She projected the "empty" body by making a face out of the torso (figs. 178-179). This is not unusual for emotionally disturbed individuals, and at times such a person may draw a number of heads telescoping out of each other. Her tree has the typical single-line trunk and a lack of support below (fig. 181).

Figure 178.   Drawing by Paula, 16 years

Figure 179.   Person by Paula, 16 years

Figure 180.   House by Paula, 16 years

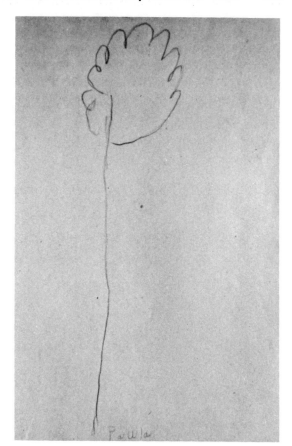

Figure 181.   Tree by Paula, 16
years.

Thelma, a twelve-year-old girl, drew and cut out the head in figure 182. It,
too, represents the concept of the head alone being the entire body-self. The
hands cover the eyes suggesting that she is not willing to see and experience
self.

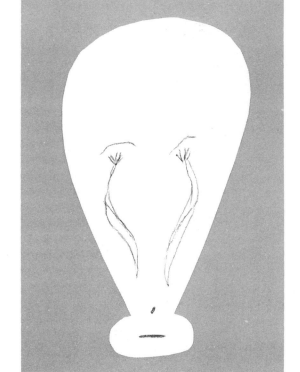

Figure 182.   Head by Thelma,
12 years.

importance placed upon the face cannot be overemphasized in the work emotionally disturbed individual. Bender (1952) has stated that the face is the last bodily part lost and the first identity rediscovered. Perhaps this is due to the child's first experiencing the face of the mother and being bound up in the circle which symbolizes the mother. In figure 183 we note a face drawn by Nancy who is twelve years old. As a self-identity, which in itself is all of reality that she now knows, she attempts to structure and organize it the best she can. The image, only too often, is like Humpty-Dumpty attempting to put himself back together.

Figure 183. Face by Nancy, 12 years.

Art and Psychotherapy for the Emotionally Disturbed

Too many people are afraid of the term *psychotherapy*. In our use of this term, we simply imply a strong and effective teaching geared to the needs of the child. Psychotherapy refers to helping the child mediate his difficulties, of encouraging him to identify and "work through" or resolve the basic life tasks which confront him and which have perhaps overwhelmed him. It may mean a quiet, encouraging atmosphere, or it may mean a strong shock. Motivation for art will vary only in degree and be tailored to individual need. Group-orientation is impossible for such specific teaching-therapy.

Since the specific needs of individual emotionally disturbed children vary, it is most appropriate to discuss the teaching-therapy process through the following case example.

The Case of Mary

At the time Mary was first taken under consideration, she was a very disturbed thirteen-year-old girl in a special education class. She was quite manic in behavior and was difficult to understand due to very slurred speech. She was anxious for any sign of attention and very openly displayed affection—even to a total stranger. She might at the same time call him a "bad murderer." Her activities seldom took any relationship to the rest of her classmates who, for the most part, were of mentally deficient etiology. Her prime interest appeared to be in a huge insect collection which she kept closely under control in bottles. At the slightest interest on the part of a visitor, she would dump all of the contents of all of the bottles out on her table. She would then express her affection for each member, dead or alive, by picking it up and caressing and kissing it. Cockroach or fly, there was little difference, for she gently expressed her affection for each one without discrimination.

Mary was born when her mother was in her early twenties. Her father deserted the mother during the pregnancy and, therefore, he has never seen his daughter. At birth the child was normal in all visible respects, but the mother gave her almost immediately to the care of the grandmother. After a few months, the grandmother passed her back to the mother who for a number of years carried on a series of relationships with various men. She neglected Mary in most respects. Mary was often locked in a closet while her mother's male companions were visiting. Her nutrition was extremely poor as is indicated by her extremely carious teeth. The welfare authorities finally removed her from the mother, along with a younger brother who was born to the mother two years after Mary. Mary since has lived in a succession of foster homes.

Proper assessment of a child like Mary is very difficult. Her Goodenough score yielded a mental age of six and a half years, but she was suspected to be a very intelligent person. Most other tests were impossible to administer to her. An intimate relationship which used art as a primary means of communication was formed with her. She centered most of her energy in art expression upon a monster figure by the name of "Shawmite" (fig. 184). She repeated the drawing of Shawmite, with little variation, over and over again for several weeks. Her description of him was always the same: She loved him and wanted to be with him, but he was coming to get her and drown her in the water where he lives. She would get very excited in telling about her monster who was also known as the "bad murderer."

The actual figure of Shawmite is composed of a basic mouth, which could as well be appendages of some sort, and two eyes which are basically vertical

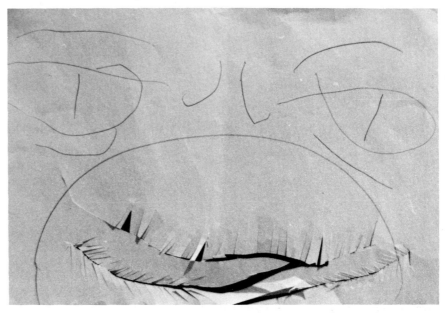

Figure 184.   "Shawmite" by Mary, 13 years

lines in a circle. The eye form was often the basis of other insects or mandala-like figures (fig. 185), and it was felt that this particular form had special significance for Mary since it symbolized her relationship of being bound up with and dependent upon the mother. It is the typical drawing of a two- to three-year-old child (see fig. 13).

Figure 185. "Eyes" by Mary, 13 years.

Great care was exercised in an effort to extend Mary's reference of experience that the repressed instinctual forces of the unconscious mind might be released from conscious control. Her story and drawings suggest a child seeking emotional birth, a birth that she is afraid to encounter because that encounter must be with a painful reality. She is desirous to be born, but is afraid. She must be encouraged. Materials were used which would enable an elaboration of the projection—large butcher paper which could be torn, cardboard, and other three-dimensionally suggestive materials.

About this time it was decided to dramatize the story she had so continuously repeated in order to provide greater contact with the real power in the symbolical context. A tub was filled with water, and as the faucet continued to flow, she was carried in as if the Shawmite would now "rub her out." She jumped from the therapist's arms and ran from the room shouting in a now clear and unaffected voice, "Help teacher, Help! Will he get out? *Will* he get out?" It was clear, now, that the eye did symbolize herself bound up in the context of the mother and desiring birth. One day shortly afterward she drew her eye to cover a whole sheet of paper and said, "People are born out of the eye."

It was not long after this that she started producing fetal horses as a self-image and as a departure from the previous monster form. She still called them Shawmites though the horse character is obvious (fig. 186). Symbolically the horse is the more primitive unconscious self. We even speak of a bad trip into the unconscious as a "night*mare*." In regard to the image of the horse in birth, one often sees Neptune, with his trident, driving the horses up out of the water.

One day Mary was given a large ice cream carton, and she tore it into the horselike form seen in figure 187. A beautiful aesthetic form of this quality indi-

Figure 186. Fetal Horse by Mary, 13 years

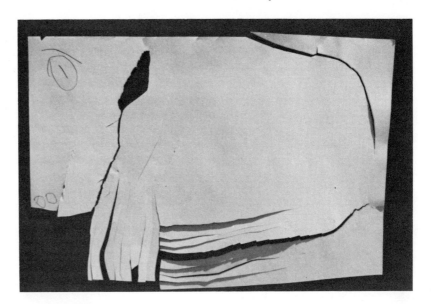

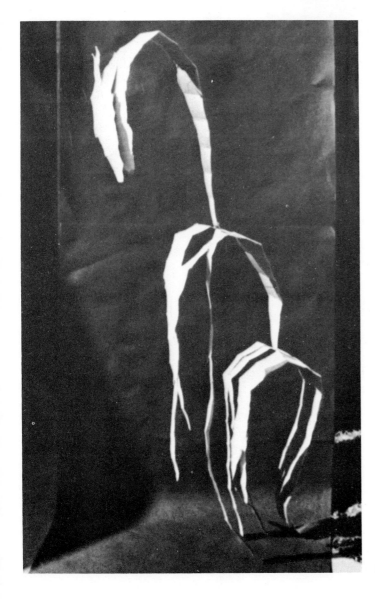

Figure 187. "Shawmite" by Mary, 13 years

cates what can arise from the disturbed personality. Over a period of time there was noticeable improvement in Mary's behavior as her reference was gradually extended through art motivation. She had stopped wetting her bed and was now very often participating in class activities, especially games. She has far to travel but could yet, even at her age, begin to interact with reality to a great and meaningful degree—if we would provide the proper encouragement. Being left to emotionally and psychically die from the moment of birth was a cruel atrocity performed upon her person, but she has survived to some degree, and her fine innate potential offers hope.

REFERENCES

BENDER, LAURETTA. *Child Psychiatric Techniques.* Springfield, Ill.: Charles C Thomas, Publisher, 1952.

CROWL, MARIANNE. "The Use of Art in Personality Evaluation: A Case Study of an Emotionally Disturbed Adolescent Boy." Unpublished master's thesis, Sacramento State College, 1968.

FRANKENSTEIN, CARL. *Psychopathy.* New York: Grune and Stratton, Inc., 1959.

JAKAB, IRENE, ed. *Psychiatry and Art.* Basel/New York: S. Karger Co., 1966.

——— *Psychiatry and Art Vol. 2: Art Interpretation and Art Therapy.* Basel/New York: S. Karger Co., 1969.

KANNER, LEO. *Child Psychiatry.* Springfield, Ill.: Charles C Thomas, Publisher, 1966.

KRAMER, EDITH. *Art Therapy in a Children's Community.* Springfield, Ill.: Charles C Thomas, Publisher, 1958.

LEVY, D. M. *Maternal Overprotection.* New York: Columbia University Press, 1943.

NAUMBURG, MARGARET. *Psychoneurotic Art: Its Function in Psychotherapy.* New York: Grune and Stratton, Inc., 1953.

——— *Schizophrenic Art: Its Meaning in Psychotherapy.* New York: Grune and Stratton, Inc., 1950.

——— *Studies of the "Free" Art Expression of Behavior Problem Children and Adolescents as a Means of Diagnosis and Therapy.* Nervous and Mental Diseases Monograph, New York: Grune and Stratton, Inc., 1947.

PASTO, TARMO. *The Space-Frame Experience in Art.* New York: A. S. Barnes and Co., Inc., 1965.

PICKFORD, R. W. *Studies of Psychiatric Art.* Springfield, Ill.: Charles C Thomas, Publisher, 1967.

PLOKKER,, J. H. *Art from the Mentally Disturbed.* Boston: Little, Brown and Co., 1964.

ROTHENBERG, MIRA. "The Rebirth of Johnny." *Harpers,* February 1960.

SCHILDER, PAUL. *The Image and Appearance of the Human Body.* New York: International Universities Press, 1950.

WITKIN, HERMAN; LEWIS, H. B.; HERTZMAN, M.; MACHOVER, K.; MEISSNER, P. BRETNALL; and WAPNER, S. *Personality Through Perception: An Experimental and Clinical Study.* New York: Harper and Brothers, 1954.

Case Examples of Multiple Impairment 6

While the basic purpose of our discussion has been to present through art a reference for discernment and therapy of specific types of exceptional children, it is also necessary to recognize that many children will, to some degree, suffer multiple involvement with these particular impairments. It is not unusual to find a child with neurological handicap who is mentally deficient as well, and perhaps orthopedically involved too. The criteria previously mentioned as characteristic of the art of the child will remain as a valid tool in evaluating impairment for the multiple-handicapped child. To illustrate the use of art for such a purpose, two cases of emotionally disturbed children will be presented.

Jimmy, Fifteen Years

When Jimmy's drawings were first observed, his more obvious problem of mental deficiency was not detected as the observer viewed the drawings without first seeing him or having knowledge of his age. Jimmy suffers mental deficiency from Down's syndrome but appears alert and could almost be called hyperactive. This, along with a great deal of aggressiveness, makes him a very unusual boy. Typically he would be expected to be slow, congenial, and shy at fifteen years of age, but he is none of these.

His first drawing (fig. 188) is a type of self-image, with the expected homunculus forms of the child with Down's syndrome, but there is an obvious "deification" of self by placing a rainbow over the head. The body is an effeminate "vaselike" form. We might also notice the aggression suggested in the teeth. His first attempt, to the right of the major figure, is purple, and all of these

Figure 188. Self-image by Jimmy, 15 years.

signs together would tend to point to a paranoid reactor, a highly unlikely circumstance for a boy with Down's syndrome. Yet, this is exactly the situation. Jimmy is actually more active and extroverted than we would expect because his behavior is more tuned to his paradox of sexual role-identification than to his mental deficiency. In fact, he perfectly expresses the dilemma in his naïve and thoroughly unconscious manner.

Jimmy's parents are divorced, and he lives with his mother. She fulfills her need of affection through him, and as a result he has identified strongly in and through her person. Behind such a relationship, however, lurks his hostility toward her, for as a final course he ultimately wishes to be a man. His identity fits perfectly the paranoid image of the Mother Goose rhyme:

> Peter, Peter, Pumpkin Eater,
> Had a wife and couldn't keep her.
> He put her in a pumpkin shell,
> And there he kept her very well.

In figure 189 we see that image projected in Jimmy's art. He is the man but also the mother as is symbolized in the pumpkin image. If he would marry, he would not adjust to his wife until he had put her in the projected "mother" image of himself; he would treat her according to the threat he feels from his own unconscious. We see this portrayed even more viciously in figure 190 where he takes on a devil character. His hostility is clearly in evidence.

Figure 189. Self-image by Jimmy, 15 years

Figure 190. Self-image by Jimmy, 15 years.

In figure 191 the cross form contains two interesting subjects which very well clarify the deeper meaning of the form. The horizontal member was labeled a "house" by Jimmy, and he called the vertical member "an elevator." It is essentially a boy attempting to rise above, and thus subordinate, his mother.

Figure 191. "Elevator and House" by Jimmy, 15 years

In figure 192 he drew a purple spearlike tree growing from a yellow rectangular ground, a clear picture of a sexually confused boy with his origin in a masculine mother.

Jimmy is a very confused boy, and because he lacks the finer rationale of a normal child, he has difficulty in organizing himself in the context of his environment. In figure 193 we note the defensive barrier forms which symbolically indicate his protective character. If he is defeated, he will sulk and become very negative in attitude. In figures 194 and 195 we note his despair and nihilism. Like most paranoid reactors, he will tend to express himself in a dark hole— a black circle or rectangle—when defeated. In figure 194 the rectangle is black with a red form, suggesting a human figure, in the center. In figure 195 the circular "house" is black and blue and purple—like a bruise.

Figure 192. Tree by Jimmy, 15 years.

Figure 193. House by Jimmy, 15 years.

Figure 194. Drawing by Jimmy, 15 years

Figure 195. Drawing by Jimmy, 15 years

Judy, Eight Years

Judy at eight years of age was a very quiet third-grader who never expressed emotion. She was neat and performed each academic requirement with extreme thoroughness. She was noted as being preoccupied of mind, and though her reading skills were sufficient, she had very poor recall and comprehension.

One day the teacher asked the class to draw "The Most Beautiful Thing" and Judy responded with a drawing of a gas station pump (fig. 196). At this the teacher referred Judy for evaluation. We note that the pump is actually a self-image with the station itself serving as a fence or barrier form for protection. The pump has small legs, a skirt, and a face with a number one and a number two drawn on the face. The face is vermillion with a blue line around it, while the figure itself is red. The pump image suggests that she is identifying strongly with a mechanical object and that she is essentially mechanical herself. Her poor ego-structure calls for the organizational protection of the fence form with its sharply pointed corners.

Figure 196. "Gas Station" by Judy, 8 years

Judy was asked next to draw the house, tree, and person figures which were found to additionally suggest emotional disturbance (figs. 197 and 198). Her house had no windows, was colored a cold brown, and had sharp points at the top like her gas station. It was suspected, from the typical symbolism of the house, that her own mother is represented in this form. The self-image was colored a masculine red with small, weak arms and barely visible hands. The tree (fig. 198) was split down the middle and thus suggested the ambivalency of the cross form. The top of the tree had a hard defensive shell around a meticulously organized interior which was significant as a structured gridlike form. From the drawings, it was suspected that Judy was much closer to her father than to her mother and that she was having great difficulty in resolving the ego-identification of self-in-the-environment.

At a conference the parents stated that Judy was indeed closer to her father since he had taken care of her during her first year of life while the mother worked. Twin boys had been born into the family at the time Judy was nearing her third birthday, and this, too, had turned her to her father for attention, as mother was very busy with the infants. Therapy measures were instituted according to what was believed to be a purely functional disturbance.

Figure 197. Person and House by Judy, 8 years.

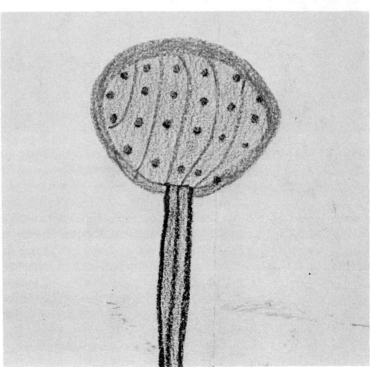

Figure 198. Tree by Judy, 8 years

During the school year Judy became constantly more rigid and organizational. Her art (figs. 199 and 200) reflected this structuring. She could not wait to leave school at the end of the day, it seemed, and often had her coat on a half hour before dismissal.

Figure 199. Person by Judy, 8 years

Figure 200. Flower by Judy, 8 years

At the end of her third-grade year, she produced a second H-T-P drawing series (figs. 201, 202, and 203). The human figure was highly stylized and looked like a mechanical robot. The tree, like the previous gas station pump, was structured with a barrier form. The house revealed a new factor. The roof had a very regular pattern in the structured form on the right side, but a very disorganized pattern on the left. This suggested a bodily imbalance and hence neurological handicap. The parents were again called, and they replied that she had suffered encephalitis at just a few weeks of age and had been placed on medication until about school age. They added that she had just suffered a cerebral seizure. She was given a thorough physical examination and placed back on medication. Her emotional disturbance had a deeper and more significant neurological etiology.

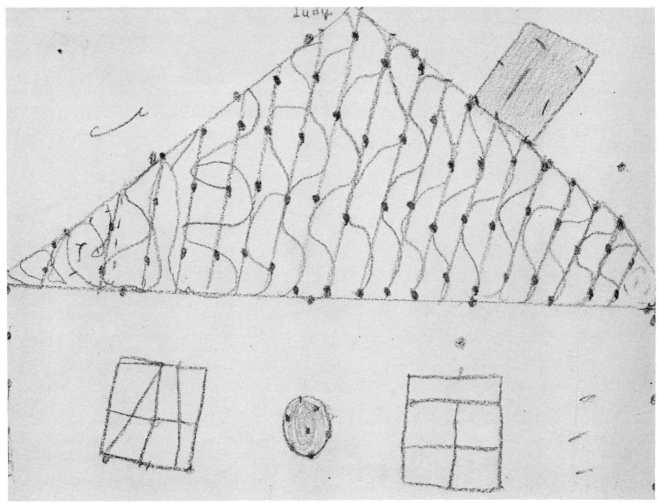

Figure 201. House by Judy, 8 years

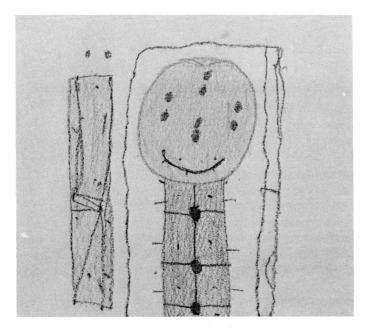

Figure 202. Tree by Judy, 8 years

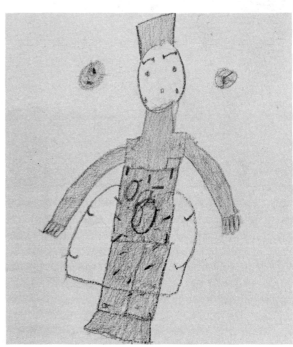

Figure 203. Person by Judy, 8 years

above left: **Figure   204.**   House by Judy, 9 years

above: **Figure 205.**   Person by Judy, 9 years

left: **Figure 206.**   Self-image by Judy, 9 years

The following year her condition tended to deteriorate even though medication continued. While the structuring of the forms persisted, the space-time orientation of the body began to fragment. Rotation to the right (figs. 204, 205, and 206) was evidenced to some degree in all of her work.

Signs of the loss of physiological identity are evident in the human figure drawings. In figure 205 the person throwing a ball is drawn by the use of small dashes, and the hands are small starlike forms. In figure 206, a self-image, Judy draws the figure with a chest-of-drawers neck and, by that means, suggests the cutting off of the psychic head from the physical body. Notice the double pupils in the eyes and the balancing from the center as evidenced in the symmetry which extends outside of the body to two vertical marks. These marks indicate a desperate attempt to "balance" or maintain one's self in the temporal space of the environment.

After Judy's fourth-grade year, the family moved and no further records of her progress have been made available.

Abstract-symbolic stage, 20
Adolescent
    art, 20, 21, 44-46
    sensitivity to physical status, 64
Affective function, 4, 11
Aggression, *see* Behavior
Anima, 4-5, *also see* Unconscious, anima
Animus, 4-5, *also see,* Unconscious, animus
Aphasia, 73
Archetype, *see* Symbol, archetype
Arnheim, R., 21, 22, 46
Art
    activities, 60-62, 88, 90
    aesthetics, 22, 33, 39, 46, 62, 84, 88, 90, 128
    crystalline character of, 114
    decorative character of, 23
    expressionism, 20
    form, 22, 46, *also see* Form
    impressionism, 20
    paleolithic, 18, 21
    realism, 23, 43
    reflective device, 3, 8, 17, 18, 94
    relationship to intelligence, *see* Intelligence
Asymmetry in drawings, 72
Auditory handicap, *see* Hearing impairment
Autistic, 94

Baldwin, J., 18, 46
Barnes, E., 19, 46
Barrier forms, *see* Emotionally disturbed characteristics in
    art
Baseline in child art, 37, 39, 43
Behavior
    aggressive, 103, 118, 120, 131
    cycle, *see* Reality structuring, chart of
    passive, 120
Behaviorists, 3
Bender, L., 21, 22, 46, 63, 70-71, 92, 126, 130
Bible, 12-13
Biological substrate, 13
Blind, *see* Visual, handicap
Body
    detached from, *see* Disassociation
    injury of, *see* Hearing impairment, Neurological impair-
        ment, Orthopedic handicap, and Visual handicap
    significance in creative personality, 6
    significance in reality structuring and maintenance, 6, 8,
        11, 114-126
    vehicle for experiencing, 6, 57, 64-68, 91
Body-image
    as expressed in art, 8, 64-67, 70-83
    definition of, 6, 8
Brain, 4
    capability of, 52, 54
    dysfunction of, *see* Neurological handicap

Britsch, G., 21, 46
Buck, J., 17, 70-71, 92
Burt, C., 20, 39, 46
Butterfly, *see* Symbol subjects

Castration, 80, 107, 108
Centers, L., and Centers, R., 65, 93
Cerebral
    damage, *see* Neurological handicap
    palsy, 68, 86
    seizure, 138
Child art
    also see, Abstract-symbolic stage, Dawning realism stage,
        Pre-schematic stage, Schematic stage, Scribbling stage,
        and Storytelling stage
    developmental stages of, 18-46
    mental concepts, 18, 19, 21, 32-33, 56, 57, 90
Child study era, 18
Chrystostom, J., 10
Circle, 24, 54, 96-102, *also see,* Scribbling, circular, and
    Symbol and form
Cirlot, J., 13, 17
Cizek, F., 20
Clark, A., 19, 46
Closure, 22, 70, 73
Cohn, R., 71, 72, 93
Color, *see* Symbol and color
Communication
    brain, function in, 52
    center for reality structuring, *see* Personality, as center of
        reality structuring and maintenance
    distortions in process, 68, 94
    significance of somatic function, 6, *also see* Body, vehicle
        for experiencing
    spirit as vehicle for, 10-11
Concept, *see* Child art, mental concepts
Concrete operations, 24, 39
Consciousness
    dreams, 12-13
    motion, 11, 12
    operation of mind, 4
Contrasexual image, 4, 103, *also see* Unconscious, anima
    and animus
Creativity, 6
Cross, *see* Symbol and form, cross
Crowl, M., 108, 130

Dawning realism stage in child art, 21
Deafness, *see* Hearing impairment
Defensiveness, 120
Dependency
    upon parent, 23, 24, 26, 46, 52, 57, 95, 96, 128
    visual, 23, 43
Descriptive symbolism, 20, 39
Diabetes insipidus, 73

Dilantin, 78, 80
Disassociation, 6-7, 94, 114-126, 135-140
Discipline, 31, 74
Distortion of form in drawing, 21, 22, 56, 65, 72
Down's syndrome, 51, 54, 131-135
Draw-a-Man Test, 21, 65, 70-71, 127, *also see* Intelligence
    and art
Dreams
    somatic origin of, 12
    soul origin of, 12
    sources of origin, 12-13
    spirit origin of, 13
Drug abuse, 98, 120-121
Dysfunction of brain, 68-88

Effeminate, 82, 108, 131
Ego, 24, 30-31, 32, 46, 55, 96, 137
    disturbance of, *see* Emotional disturbance
Eidetic image, 21
Electroencephalograph, 7, 77, 80
Emotion, 4
    flexibility, 6, 52, 64
    relationship of color to, 56
Emotional disturbance, 7, 13, 91, 94-130, 131-140
    among children with hearing impairments, 90, 92
    behavior, 94
    disassociation in, 6-7, 94, 114-126, 135-140
    etiology, 94-96
Emotionally disturbed characteristics in art
    barrier forms, 14, 118, 134, 136, 138
    concentric linear structures, 96-98, 115, 122
    double pupils in eye, 140
    "empty" bodily forms, 96, 101, 122, 124
    head detached from body, 6-7, 94, 114-126, 135-140
    rigid symmetry of form, 122, 135-140
    stylized heads, 96, 122, 135-140
    symbols, *see* Symbol subjects
Encephalitis, 138
Endogenous, *see* Mental deficiency, labels and classification
Environment
    organization of, 30, 114-126
    physical, 4, 11, 57
Exaggeration of form in drawing, 21, 23, 56, 65
Exhibitionism, 110, 112, 113
Existentialism, 13
Exogenous, 51, 69, 84, *also see* Neurological Handicap,
    labels
Extrovert, 22, 23, 43, 46

Familial, 51, 69, *also see* Mental deficiency, labels and clas-
    sification
Feebleminded, *see* Mental deficiency, labels and classifica-
    tion
Feminine
    personality, *see* Personality, feminine
    puppets, 8-9
Fetal image, 96, 128
Field-dependent vs. field-independent, *see* Perception

Figure-ground, 21, 84-88, *also see* Gestalt, organization
Flores, A., 88-89, 93
Fold-over view, 21, 40
Forgery, 109
Form distortion, exaggeration, and omission in physical im-
    pairment, 64-88
Formal operations, 24
Frankenstein, C., 95
Freud, S., 103
Functional disturbance, definition and etiology, 94

Gaitskell, C., 54, 63
Games, manipulative, 57, 92
Gang age stage, *see* Dawning realism stage in child art
Gestalt
    function of brain, 69
    organization, 55, 56, 70, 84, 88, 90
    psychology, 18, 21, 22, 24, 26, 33, 96
Goldtein, K., 70, 93
Goodenough, F., 21, 46, 52, 63, 65, 70-71, 127
Group activity, 126, 130
    puppets, 60

Handicap
    auditory, *see* Hearing impairment
    definition of, 64
    mental deficiency, *see* Mental deficiency
    neurological, *see* Neurological handicap
    orthopedic, *see* Orthopedic handicap
    visual, *see* Visual handicap
Hanvik, L., 70, 93
Haptic, *see* Perception, visual-haptic types
Harris, D., 21, 46
Hartlaub, G., 21, 46
Head, H., 8, 17, 69, 93
Hearing impairment, 64, 90-92
Heavy line pressure in drawing, 72
Hebb, D., 69
Homicide, 82, 113
Homosexuality, 110-112, 113
Hostility, 103, 118, 132
House-Tree-Person Test, 8, 21, 52, 76, 80-81, 82, 109, 136,
    138
    administration of, 9

Ideoplastic art, 20, 39
Impressionistic art, 20
Infantile autism, 94
Intelligence, 51-52, 53, 54, 70-71, 77, 79, 116, 118, 127
Intelligence and art, 21, 46, 68
Introvert, 22, 23, 43, 46

Jaensch, E., 21, 46
Jolles, I., 17, 70-71, 93
Jung, C., 13, 17, 22, 23, 24

Kanner, L., 94, 130
Kant, I., 13

Kellogg, R., 21, 22, 46
Kinesthetic, 21, 22, 32, 39, 56-57, 70
   passive type, 57
   relationship to space-time orientation, 94
Koffka, K., 22
Koppitz, E., 70

LeBelle, J., 13
Lehtinen, L., 74, 93
Levenstein, S., 20, 32, 46
Levy, D., 95, 130
Lichtwark, A., 18, 46
Line, 38, 39
   perspective, 56
Lowenfeld, V., 21, 23, 24, 25, 32, 39, 40, 43, 47, 65, 88,
   90, 93
Lukens, H., 19, 47

Machover, K., 17, 71
Maitland, L., 19, 47
Mandala, 22, 23, 73, 128
Manipulative
   games, 57, 92
   skills, 60, 62
Martorana, A., 65
Masculine
   personality, *see* Personality, masculine
   puppets, 9
Maternal indolence, rejection, and overindulgence, 95, *also*
    see Dependency, upon parent
Maury, A., 12
McCarty, S., 21
Medication
   abuse of, *see* Drug abuse
   effects of, 76-83, 140
Mental concept, *see* Child art, mental concepts
Mental deficiency, 51, 69, 84, 127, 131-135
   capability in, 51
   concepts, 52, 56
   definition of, 51-52
   etiology, 51
   labels and classification, 51, 52, 55, 56
Michal-Smith, H., 71, 93
Mind, 4
   as battlefield, 10, 11, 128, 132
   conscious operation of, 4, 64
   deficient status of, 52
   distortion of, 64, 94
   motion experience of, 12
   unconscious operation of, 4, 64, 128
Mira, E., 22, 47
Mongolism, *see* Down's syndrome
Mother, overprotection, *see* Dependency, upon parent
Mother Goose, 14, 39, 132
Motion
   expression in art, 20, 21, 22
   relationship to time and space, 6, 11, 37, 56, 57
Motivation, 17, 42, 56, 57-59, 65, 90, 126, 130

Motor activity
   coordination, 52
   in neurological handicap, *see* Neurological handicap
   production of form, 22, 24
   stereotyped, 94
Murder, *see* Homicide

Neptune, *see* Symbol subjects
Neurological handicap, 51, 64, 68-88, 131, 135-140
   behavior, 70-71, 74, 77, 79
   drawing characteristics, 70, 71, 73, 74, 76, 77, 79, 80-81,
    138, 140
   labels, 69-70
   motor activity in, 70-78, 79, 84-88
   perception of motion, 69-70
   projection of body-image, 70-83

Object-ground relationship, *see* Figure-ground
Oedipus complex, 103
Omission or delineation of forms, 21, 23, 56, 65
Orthopedic handicap, 64-68
Overlapping, 43, 56

Paralysis of body, 64-65, 66
Paranoid reactor, 30, 82, 103-114, 120, 122, 131-140
Passive, *see* Behavior, passive
Passive and aggressive behavior, 120
Pasto, T., 24, 26, 47, 130
Perception
   coherent-incoherent types, 84
   field-dependent vs. field-independent types, 23-24, 43,
    46, 105
   handicap, *see* Neurological handicap
   process of, 6, 21, 57, 90
   visual-haptic types, 23, 43, 46, 56, 88-90
Perseveration, 72
Personality
   basis of health, 7
   center of structured reality, 4, 11
   creative, 6
   definition and basic characteristics, 4, 5
   feminine, 4, 24, 30, 82, 114
   function of, 3, 11, 17
   masculine, 4, 30
   spirit communication to, 10-13
Pfiester, H., 70, 93
Phallus, 107, 108, 112
Physical
   basis for spiritual communication, 10
   component in experiencing, 4, 8, 11, 24, 34, 56, 57
   games, *see* Games, manipulative
   origin of dreams, *see* Dreams, somatic origin of
   projection in puppets, 8
   senses, 4, 11
Physioplastic art, 20
Piaget, J., 24, 39, 47
Posture of body, 6, 8, *also see* Schemata, of body

Pre-schematic, 24, 32, 57
Primitive wholes in drawing, 72
Projection
  body-image in neurological handicap, *see* Neurological handicap, projection of body-image
  of awareness in art, 6, 8, 17, 64-65, 66-67
Proximity of forms, 22, 70
Psyche, 10
  birth and growth of, 95
  death of, 130
  disturbance of, 94
  function of, 17
  projection in puppets, 8-9
  suicide, 7
Psychotherapy, 126

Rational
  center, 3, 11
  function, 4, 11, 94
Read, H., 8, 17, 21, 22, 47
Reality
  detachment from, 94-95
  essence of, 4, 11
  temporal, 3, 4, 11
  transcendent, 10-17
Reality structuring
  affective function, *see* Affective function
  body as basis of, *see* Body, as basis for experiencing
  chart of, 11
  deficient experiencing, 52
  disturbance of, *see* Emotional disturbance
  levels of awareness, *see* Mind, conscious and unconscious operation
  motion, *see* Motion, time and space
  personality as center of, *see* Personality, as center of reality structuring and maintenance
  physical senses, *see* Physical senses, component in experiencing
  self-consciousness, *see* self-awareness
  soul, *see* Soul
  spirit as basis for communication, *see* Spirit, communication component, definition
  symbol, *see* Symbol, Symbol and color, Symbol and form, Symbol subjects
  temporal reality, *see* Temporal reality
  time-space, *see* Space, relation to motion
  transcendent reality, *see* Transcendent reality
  will, *see* Will
Redrawing and erasing, 72
Representational symbol, 21, 32, *also see* Child art, mental concepts
Responsive function, 4
Retarded
  mildly, 52
  moderately, 52, 55
  severely, 52, 55, 57-58
Reznikoff, M., and Tomblen, D., 71
Rhythm, 22, 23, 39, 56, 57, 70

Ricci, C., 18, 47
Rothenberg, M., 95, 130
Ruben, E., 84, 93
Running away, 98

Schaefer-Simmern, H., 21, 47
Schemata,
  child art, 19
  of body, 8, 19
Schematic stage in child art, 24, 39-43, 46, 54-56
Schilder, P., 8, 17, 130
Schizophrenic, 94, 95
  ambulating, 94, 95
  paranoid, 108
Scribbling, 18-21, 24-27, 57, 84
  circular, 26-27, 54, 55, 89, 128
  disordered, 25, 54
  longitudinal, 25
  naming of, 24
Seeman, E., 22, 47
Self-awareness, 4, 117
  expression in art, 8, 26, 32, 43, 88, 107, 131
Senses and communication, 6, 11, 13, 17, 57, 88
Sensitize, 17, 20, 57, 60-62
  to body, 122
Sensory experiencing, 20, 22, 24, 25, 26, 46
Sexual
  expression in art, 8-9, 132
  identification, 4, 24, 30, 44, 46, 55, 94-126, 136
  image, 4
  inversion, 103, 110
Simplification, 72
Social
  adaptation, 55, 69, 70
  awareness, 21, 43, 44, 46, 64
  confidence, 56, 60
  participation, 23, 37, 39
Soma
  appearance of, 4, 5
  definition and basic character of, 4, 8, 11, 17
  dream, 12
  orthopedic impairment, 64-68
  projection in puppets, 8, 9
  serving personality, 6
Soul, 5
  dream, 12
Space, 3, 4
  depth representation, 20, 23, 90
  organization of, 33
  perception of, 24, 69-70
  relation to motion, 6, 37, 69
  tactual, 23
Space-frame, 24
Spirit
  communication, 10-17
  component, 10-17
  definition, 10
Stealing, 82

Stern, W., 20, 47
Storytelling stage in art, 19-20
Strauss, A., and Werner, H., 84, 93
Sturge-Weber syndrome, 86
Suicide, 82, 98, 113
   psychic, 6, 109
Sully, J., 19, 47
Swing scribble, 24, 25, 55, *also see* Scribbling, longitudinal
Symbol
   anima and animus, 4, 5, 10, *also see,* Unconscious, anima
      and animus
   archetype, 13-14
   body-image, 8
   significance in child art, 19, 20, 23, 39
   significance in dreams and art, 10-17
   universal language, 10-13, 95
Symbol and color
   black, 99, 119, 134
   blue, 99, 118, 134
   brown, 136
   green, 118-119
   orange, 118-119
   purple, 99, 118-119, 131, 134
   red, 136
   yellow, 134
Symbol and form, 24, 95-130
   circle, 24, 26-27, 46, 54, 95-102
   cross, 24, 27-30, 46, 54, 96, 103-114
   rectangle, 24-30, 36, 46, 96, 114-126, 137
Symbol subjects
   arms, 98, 118
   belt buckle, 105, 122
   birds, 108, 116
   branch, 82
   breasts, 105
   butterfly, 5, 100
   buttons, 98, 115
   chin, 105, 113
   clothing, 82
   dinosaur, 108
   door, 12
   ear, 112, 115
   earth, 14
   eyelashes, 115
   eyes, 113, 120, 125, 127-128
   face, 126
   feet, 98, 112
   fence, 14, 118, 134, 136, 138
   fingers, 82, 115
   flowers, 14, 15
   ground, 14
   hair, 44
   hands, 98, 112, 122
   head, 92, 107, 120, 122, 124, 125, 140
   horse, 5, 128
   house, 14, 52, 133
   jaw, 113
   lizard, 108

   moon, 14
   mountain, 14, 105, 120
   mouth, 52, 127
   neck, 107, 108, 109, 122, 140
   neptune, 128
   nose, 112
   pumpkin, 132
   rabbit, 110, 116
   shoe laces, 80
   shoes, 105
   squirrel hole, 15, 82
   sun, 13, 122
   teeth, 113, 115, 131
   thumb, 107
   tongue, 112
   trunk, 116
   umbilicus, 52
   water, 14, 127
Symbolists, 20
Symmetry in art, 22, 103-144, 120
Synchronism, 13

Tactual
   motor test, 84
   sensitivity, 23, 56, 60-61, 90
   space, 23
Temporal reality, 3, 4, 6, 10, 11, 17
   space, 3, 10, 11, 57, 69-70, 84-88, 90, 91-92, 94, 114-126,
      140
   time, 3, 10, 11, 21, 57, 84-88, 90, 91-92, 94
Therapy, 17, 131, 137
Time
   relation to motion, 6, 69-70, 84-88, 90, 91-92, 94, 114-
      126, 140
   symbol, 10
Transcendent reality, 13

Unconscious
   anima and animus, 4, 5, 10
   communication, 10-17
   dreams, 12-13
   horse image as primitive, 5, 128
   operation of mind, 4
   projection in puppets, 8-9

Vaginal symbol, 112, 113
Vernier, C., 71, 93
Verworn, M., 20, 39, 47
Viola, W., 20, 47
Visual
   dependency, *see* Perception, field-dependent vs. field-
      independent types
   handicap, 64, 88-90
   perception, 22, 23, 43, 46, 57, 88-90
Visual-motor control, 25
Visual-Motor Gestalt Test, 22, 70, 77
Visual-motor sense, 46

Visual-motor test, 84
Visual-perceptual handicap, 64, 68-88, *also see* Neurological handicap
Voyeurism, 110

Weak synthesis of parts in drawing, 72
Werner, H., and Thuma, B., 84, 93

Will, 4, 11
Wish fulfillment
    dreams, 12
Withdrawal from body, *see* Disassociation
Witkin, H., 23-24, 43, 47, 105, 130

X-ray view in art, 18, 21, 40

DATE DUE

JUL 1 4 1993			
JUL 3 0 1993			
OCT 1 1 1993			
NOV 2 2 1993			
JUN 0 8 1994			
DEC 0 6 1994			
FEB 2 1 1996			
JUN 1 4 1999			